BBC QUIZBOOKS
SUPERSCOT

To Sorcha
With Love.
Gran.
24.11.88.

D1352316

Superscot

compiled by
Donald W. Stewart

with a foreword by
Jane Franchi

BBC BOOKS

BBC QUIZBOOKS

Telly Addicts
Masterteam
Brain of Sport
First Class
Trivia Test Match
Superscot
Telly Addicts 2
Food & Drink
The Archers
Beat the Teacher

Published by BBC Books,
a division of BBC Enterprises Limited
Woodlands, 80 Wood Lane, London W12 0TT

First published 1988

© British Broadcasting Corporation 1988

Foreword © Jane Franchi 1988

ISBN 0 563 20683 7

Set in 10/11 Plantin by
Wilmaset, Birkenhead, Wirral
Printed and bound in Great Britain by
Richard Clay Ltd, Bungay, Suffolk

CONTENTS

FOREWORD

There are two things I can always be certain of in
Superscot . . .

- at the pre-programme questions check, somebody is
  going to say, 'That question's too difficult'
- when it's asked in the programme, the fingers of all
  four contestants will pounce on the buzzers.

It works in reverse too. As sure as fate, if those of us
behind the scenes think a question's insulting in its
simplicity, it'll be the one that draws the blank looks on
the programme.

So when I'm accosted (usually with a loaded trolley in
the supermarket) by a viewer who says I was 'hard on
that nice young man second from the left', with a
particularly difficult question, I just smile quietly and
remember the earliest days of *Superscot*. That was when
the producer Charles Nairn, who devised the quiz and
who still scratches his head at the wisdom of giving me
my big chance, used to say, 'We can't call a question
difficult or easy. It's only difficult if you don't know the
answer. If you do, it's simple.'

I love *Superscot*. It's taught me so much . . . and not
just about my country and her people. I wish I could
claim to remember all the facts we get through in a series,
but at that speed it would be impossible. Even the few
that have sunk in have taught me how little I knew about
Scotland. I've had a lot to learn. I know how to
pronounce Meikleour now, thanks to several irate letters
and I'll be careful never to confuse mealie puddings with
skirlie again!

It's often the calls and letters after the programmes
which add to my knowledge. And that's something else
I've learned. Football isn't this nation's favourite sport.
Proving the question master/mistress wrong is an
audience participation pastime that can be enjoyed from
the warmth of a fireside and the comfort of an armchair.
It wins hands-down over draughty terracings.

Curiously enough, I used to find this 'get the referee syndrome' a little upsetting. But it's led to so many fascinating conversations and letters that I've come to regard it as yet another of the advantages of hosting *Superscot*.

I'm often asked (yes the boot is sometimes on the other foot) about the most precious thing I've gained from *Superscot*. I have to say it's new friends. There are the many unnamed, unsung people behind the scenes who've checked and double-checked the questions, my ear-piece, my glass of water and my monitors; there are those who have held my hand (frequently both my hands), guided me, covered the lines on my face and then lied about how much Polyfilla make-up they needed for the task. And there are the many, many viewers who have welcomed me into their homes.

But the most precious of all my new friends have to be the really important people in the programmes – the Super Scots who've made the quiz so successful – the contestants. It's always sad when, inevitably, those who have been knocked out don't come back to the panel. But we all take great pleasure in the fact that so many of them return later in the series, or even several series later, to sit in the audience and watch, surely with a tiny regret, as four others go through the thrilling grilling.

Thanks to those who have sat in the hot seats we've all found out how super Scots really are. I'm proud to be one – a Scot that is. I could never earn the full title – nae chance.

Jane Franchi

HOW TO PLAY SUPERSCOT

Three things you do *not* need to enjoy playing *Superscot* are:
- a university degree in Scottish studies
- an expert knowledge of Scots history
- the ability to recite 'Tam O'Shanter' from memory.

What you *do* need are:
- an affection for Scotland – and
- a general interest in what's going on around you in Scotland today – what's in the pop charts, who's in the news, what are the latest fashions and who's currently top of the league.

On the screen, *Superscot* has a good-humoured and down-to-earth approach to fact-finding about Scotland and the people who live here, and that atmosphere is easy to recreate at home or in a club or workplace quiz. On television there are four competitors – each playing for themselves. This book is designed so that each round can be played by two, three, four or even six people – with the presenter asking each competitor an equal number of questions from each round.

If you are presenting the quiz for two or more competitors, you may find it more fun to vary rounds between questions for individual team-members, and quick-fire rounds where the first to answer correctly wins the points. Or you can set each team a time limit of, say, two minutes and see how many questions they can answer correctly before the time is up.

Of course, it is just as much fun to test yourself on some of the rounds which have become popular with the show's million-plus viewers. You can set yourself a target number of questions to answer correctly in a round, or give yourself a time limit for each round.

Most of the questions in this book have been included in *Superscot* in recent years, but some have been specially written. For instance, the Place the Place round – on television this uses pictures of landmarks which are progressively revealed as the value of the answer goes down – has been adapted for the book so that you earn three points if you identify the mystery place from one clue (in words); two points if you need two clues; and only one point if you don't 'place the place' till you've read all three clues.

The Yes or No round, and a round about food and drink – both featured in the 1987 television series – are here in the book, along with questions about entertainment, news, sport, Scots words and phrases, and general knowledge (including jumbled-up place names to identify).

It's two points for a correct answer and one point for a near miss.

Remember, above all, that *Superscot* is not a deadly serious test of specialised knowledge. It's created so that you – like the people who prepare the television show for the screen – can have fun finding out how much you know about what's been going on in Scotland, or what Scots have been up to elsewhere. Have a 'super' time!

Donald W. Stewart

GAME 1

1   Will you see the crown jewels of Scotland at the Palace of Holyroodhouse in Edinburgh?

2   Was the song 'The Laird of Cockpen' written by Lady Nairne?

3   Did the last prime minister to represent a Scottish constituency take office in 1962?

4   Was Anne of Denmark married to King James VI?

5   Is the word 'sickerly' a Scots word for 'certainly'?

6   Is the seven of diamonds the playing card that's nicknamed 'the curse of Scotland'?

7   Does the island of Staffa lie further west than Iona?

8   Was Princess Margaret born at Glamis Castle in 1930?

9   If you visit Castle Campbell, are you in Strathclyde Region?

10 Was a Scots pint more than an imperial pint?

11 Do Kirkcudbright and Aberdeen each stand on rivers with the same name?

12 Is the Earl of Mar and Kellie the Hereditary Keeper of Stirling Castle?

1   Which musical instrument was James Scott Skinner famous for playing?

2   Which pop duo topped the hit parade in 1985 with 'There Must Be An Angel'?

3   Do you know who wrote the play *What Every Woman Knows*?

4   What was the rank and surname of the local undertaker played in the *Dad's Army* television series by the late John Laurie?

5   In song, who did Andy Stewart ask 'Where's Yer Troosers'?

6   Which royal duchess became the Patron of Scottish Opera in 1986?

7   The TRIC Awards of Scotland are presented annually. What do the initials TRIC stand for?

8   Where would you come across a 'Dashing White Sergeant'?

9   On the same theme, if you take part in a 'Dashing White Sergeant', how many people join your particular group besides yourself?

10 In February of 1987, which Scottish broadcaster celebrated the 2000th edition of his Radio Scotland programme?

11 What kind of 'gold' does that same broadcaster feature regularly on his weekend radio show?

12 A creature called Snorbitz appeared on stage at Glasgow's Theatre Royal in February, 1987. Was Snorbitz a dog?

GAME 1 PLACE THE PLACE

1 Prince Albert bought some land near here in 1852 (3
   points).
   A new building was occupied here by the Royal
   Family in 1855 (2 points).
   And in the fifteenth century the place was known as
   'Bouchmorale' (1 point).

2 Dukes of Hamilton once owned a castle with the
   same name as this island village (3 points).
   The mountain of Goatfell is nearby (2 points).
   And the village is on the east coast of the Isle of
   Arran (1 point).

3 They say St Patrick was born in this town (3 points).
   It stands where the River Leven meets the Clyde (2
   points).
   And there's a well-known view from a castle on a
   rock here (1 point).

4 Duart Castle stands on this island (3 points).
   Craignure is its main ferry port (2 points).
   And a Spanish galleon lies in the bay at the island's
   'capital' (1 point).

5 History's celebrated Appin murder trial was held in
   the courthouse of this Argyll town (3 points).
   It stands on Loch Fyne (2 points).
   And a castle sharing the town's name is the seat of
   the chief of Clan Campbell (1 point).

6 You'll find a church known as the 'Lamp of
   Lothian' in this town (3 points).
   The town once gave its name to the county where it
   stands (2 points).
   But it's now the home of East Lothian District
   Council (1 point).

7 During the Kirk's General Assembly, the Lord High Commissioner stays here each year (3 points).
There's a portrait gallery of over 100 Scots kings in the building (2 points).
And it was the scene of David Rizzio's murder (1 point).

8 On an island in this Highland loch there once stood the home of the Pope's Vicar Apostolic of Scotland (3 points).
The loch is separated from Loch Nevis by a narrow piece of land (2 points).
And it's the deepest loch in Scotland (1 point).

9 Scottish League football matches are played here at Muirton Park (3 points).
There are two parks known as 'Inches' (2 points).
And this place is called the 'Fair City' (1 point).

10 This important fishing port lies near the mouth of the River Ugie (3 points).
There's a statue of Marshal Keith in front of the Town House (2 points).
And there's a high-security prison at the town (1 point).

11 This castle was the ancestral home of the Queen Mother's father (3 points).
Its grounds are bordered by the Dean Water (2 points).
And from its battlements you can see fine views of the Vale of Strathmore (1 point).

12 This town gave its name to a type of bonnet (3 points).
An edition of Burns' poems carries the town's name too (2 points).
And the local football team plays at Rugby Park (1 point).

GAME 1 GENERAL KNOWLEDGE (1)

1 Which castle will you see on a £20 Royal Bank of Scotland note? Is is Brodick, Stirling or Edinburgh Castle?

2 Which colour is mentioned in the first verse of the metrical version of the Twenty-third psalm?

3 What's the name of Princess Alexandra's son?

4 In which county would you be if you stood on the most northerly point of the Scottish mainland?

5 To which mainland port would you normally go to catch the car ferry to Brodick on Arran?

6 Of which clan is the Duke of Atholl the chief?

7 Which name, based on the Latin for 'James', describes a supporter of the Royal Stuarts?

8 Which King James of Scotland was called 'James of the Fiery Face'?

9 In which century did the explorer David Livingstone live?

10 In children's books, on which island is Magnus MacDuff introduced to us by Lavinia Derwent?

11 If you go to the Lay Observer in Scotland, you want your complaint investigated against someone of which profession?

12 Is the Arbroath Herald a town-crier traditionally employed by the local council, a Herald of the Lord Lyon, or a local newspaper?

1   In season 1986–87, in which division of the Scottish football league did Hamilton Academicals play?

2   Douglas Young was Scotland's 1986 Commonwealth Games captain in which sport?

3   Still with the 1986 Commonwealth Games, in which sport did Jean Hill win a silver medal?

4   In March of 1987, in which sport did Scotland play an international at the Parc des Princes in Paris?

5   In which competition did Scotland's footballers play the Republic of Ireland in February of 1987?

6   Which 1987 world sporting championships were held at Coatbridge in February of 1987?

7   In Scottish league football, who are the 'Sons'?

8   In which sport have Strathmore Scorpions competed in recent years? Is it tiddlywinks, American football, or volleyball?

9   Jiggers, cleeks and sammies have been used in which sport?

10 Who won the 1982 Open Golf Championship at Troon?

11 On which island is Scotland's National Water Sports Training Centre?

12 In 1971, where did John Taylor carry out what's been described as 'the greatest conversion since St Paul'?

GAME 1 SCOTS WORDS AND SAYINGS

1   In Scotland, what is a 'thack biggin'?

2   Which children's game had a variation called 'Tippeny-Nippeny' in Scotland?

3   If you put on 'bottomless breeks', what are you wearing?

4   In superstition of the sea, fishermen traditionally never referred to certain animals by their usual name, but called them 'Sandy Campbells'. What were they?

5   Last century, what kind of marriage was known as a 'Coldstream marriage'?

6   What kind of weather would you expect at the 'gab o' May'?

7   In the north-east of Scotland, what is a 'quine'?

8   If you're told to take part in a 'diet' at a Scottish court, what will you be attending?

9   A successful product from the old Carron Works in Stirlingshire was the 'carronade'. What was it?

10 According to the Scots phrase, what's your general attitude if you 'tak the bree wi' the barm'?

11 Which bird has been known as the 'red hawk' in Scotland?

12 In place-names, what does the prefix 'Auchin' usually mean – as in Auchinleck?

GAME 1 FOOD AND DRINK

1   In Scotland, which food is jokingly known as a 'twa-eyed steak'?

2   In a riddle, what was this: 'A wee, wee house, fu', fu' of meat; Wi' neither door nor winda' tae let me in tae eat'?

3   Which colour of bun is linked with Hogmanay?

4   How did a 'clootie' dumpling get its name?

5   Once they were known as Closefish, Pinwiddies or Auchmithie Luckens. What are they called today?

6   If you were offered 'cheugh Jeans', would you wear them, eat them or plant them?

7   You must answer both parts of this question correctly to win the points: Which two vegetables would you take to make the north-east of Scotland dish of Kailkenny?

8   How old must you be before you can buy wine with your meal in a restaurant in Scotland?

9   Which fruit is called a 'grosset' in Scotland?

10   What shape are the shortbread biscuits called 'petticoat tails'?

11   Burns wrote that 'freedom and . . .' something else 'gang thegither'. What goes with freedom here?

12   In the Scots phrase which means 'the ordinary humdrum world', what goes with 'auld claes'?

1 The name of a village in north-west Sutherland is hidden in these jumbled-up letters: RED SUNS. Which village?

2 In education, can you name two of the three levels of courses leading to the new Standard Grade exams?

3 How many traffic wardens are there in Scotland . . . 500, 1000 or 2000?

4 In which Canadian city did a former Glasgow University student called James McGill found a university which is named after him?

5 Who is the Lord Keeper of the Great Seal of Scotland? Is it Prince Charles, the Secretary of State for Scotland, or the Lord Chamberlain?

6 If you cross the Forth Road Bridge on a motor bike and offer £1 for your toll, what change will you get back?

7 What kind of establishment would you link with the names of Glencorse, Redford and Fort George?

8 Which Firth of Forth island shares a name with a month of the year?

9 How many miles of public roads are there in Scotland – around 25 000 miles, 50 000 miles or 75 000 miles?

10 Which Banffshire town has been known locally as Foggieloan?

11 What's in the middle of Inverness, and also at the centre of Dunfermline and Largs?

12 Who's the famous son-in-law of Mrs Frances Shand-Kydd of the Island of Seil?

GAME 2

1 Does the verb 'to burke' mean to murder someone in the same way as the Edinburgh criminals Burke and Hare?

2 Is Prince Charles a Knight of the Thistle?

3 Is the Drummond Castle Manuscript a collection of bagpipe tunes?

4 In Scotland, was a 'trammie' someone who worked on the trams?

5 Did one of Mary Queen of Scots' husbands become the Duke of Orkney?

6 Is the town of Lochgelly in Kirkcaldy District?

7 Was the writer Compton Mackenzie born in London?

8 Is the village of Tomintoul higher than Ailsa Craig?

9 Was King Edward II's army beaten at Stirling Bridge in the year 1297?

10 An animal called Gorry arrived at Edinburgh Zoo in 1987 for a well-publicised courtship. Was Gorry a gorilla?

11 Did Ramsay MacDonald become Britain's first Labour prime minister in 1922?

12 Following royal protocol in Scotland, does the Princess Royal take precedence above the Duchess of Rothesay?

1   In which of the arts has Elaine McDonald reached the top?

2   What was the first name of the songwriter Lady Nairne?

3   In the world of variety, who was the 'tall droll'?

4   Which well-known Auntie Kathleen celebrated her ninetieth birthday in February of 1987?

5   In song, who was asked 'Or are your drums a-beating yet'?

6   Which song has the lines 'I'm only a common old working chap, As anyone here can see'?

7   Who played the male lead in the 1987 television comedy series *Tutti Frutti*?

8   Where is Britain's most northerly BBC radio station based?

9   Which square will you find in Dundee that's also in *EastEnders*?

10 Who was quoted as saying: 'Most Scots comics either belong to Glasgow, or pretend that they do'? Was it Jimmy Logan, Jack House, or Jimmy Tarbuck?

11 From which song does this line come: 'The hills are bare now, and autumn leaves lie thick and still'?

12 Which Scot wrote about his adventures at work with brothers called Siegfried and Tristan?

1 Tom Buyers has been in the headlines in the '80s as Her Majesty's Chief Inspector of . . . what?

2 Which Scottish MP became the Shadow Chancellor in 1987?

3 Which Scottish hotel was awarded five red stars by the Automobile Association in November of 1986?

4 Who is the university chancellor who became chairman of the new Standing Commission on the Scottish Economy in 1986?

5 Who became the royal patrons of the 1988 National Garden Festival in Glasgow?

6 Can you name the two cousins who supported the Earl of Inverness when he took his seat in the House of Lords in February 1987?

7 Which Secret Society attracted the interest of the Special Branch in Glasgow in February 1987?

8 Which political party conference was chaired by Charles Kennedy MP at Aberdeen in 1987?

9 In which year did Pope John Paul II visit Scotland?

10 Which Scottish bank merged with the English Williams and Glyn's bank in 1985?

11 From which Scottish organisation did Dr George Mathewson resign as chief executive in March of 1987?

12 What kind of transport was 'deregulated' in Scotland on 26 October 1986?

1   Which Lanarkshire town shares a name with two cities – one on Canada's Lake Ontario, and one on the North Island of New Zealand?

2   If you flew in a straight line from Paris to Edinburgh, would you go north-east, or north-west?

3   Which lies further south, Dundee or the city of Moscow?

4   When you buy an electric light bulb, what should remind you of a Scottish engineer born in 1736 who did pioneering work on the steam engine?

5   What kind of power is supplied by the Tummel Valley Scheme?

6   Books: what's the name of the hero of *The Thirty-nine Steps*, by John Buchan?

7   Of which country did John Buchan become Governor General (as Lord Tweedsmuir) in 1935?

8   In which Firth is the Bass Rock?

9   And in which Firth is the isle of Inchmarnock?

10   Whose supporters lost the Battle of Langside in 1568?

11   Can you name the Secretary for Scotland who went on to be Prime Minister from 1902 till 1905?

12   Which is higher, Ailsa Craig or the hill of Arthur's Seat at Edinburgh?

1   What is the 'Mo' of footballer Mo Johnston short for?

2   Besides Scotland, how many countries play in the international rugby union championship?

3   Football: what's the home town of Albion Rovers?

4   Which Scottish League football team play home games at Ochilview Park?

5   Golf: by which name did a girl, born Isabella McCorkindale in Argyll, come to be best known?

6   Which teenager raked the long-jump pit at the 1970 Commonwealth Games in Edinburgh, and ten years later became an Olympic champion as a runner?

7   The Meadowbank sports stadium at Edinburgh opened in 1970. In which year was the first athletics world record set on the track?

8   What name links *The Guinness Book of Records* itself with Scottish international sprinting?

9   Would you throw a Pentland Javelin, and if not, why not?

10 Which Scottish football team has a nickname which sounds as though the players are university teachers?

11 Which tree do the names of East Stirlingshire, Motherwell and Partick Thistle grounds have in common?

12 When the full card is played, how many matches are there on a Saturday afternoon covering the three Scottish League football divisions?

GAME 2 SCOTS WORDS AND SAYINGS

1   In Scots, if you show 'rumgumption' are you shrewd, cowardly or embarrassed?

2   What kind of information would you get from a 'waggity wa' '?

3   In the song 'John Anderson, My Jo', what does the word 'Jo' mean?

4   What would you do with a 'semmit'?

5   How many of these four words are genuine Scottish place names: Williamwood, Bettyhill, Jeantown and Ben Doon?

6   Which creature did the poet Hugh MacDiarmid describe as 'half like a bird, and half like a bogle'? Was it an owl, a pheasant or a turkey?

7   Is the girl's name Shona a form of 'Jane'?

8   Is the boy's name Neil a form of 'Nigel'?

9   In Scots, what creature is a 'pollywag'?

10   Would you wear a Scotch muffler? And if not, why not?

11   Which part of your body is your 'kyte'?

12   What's the usual name for a 'philabeg'?

GAME 2 FOOD AND DRINK

1   Which traditional Scottish food is usually boiled and then toasted?

2   Which language gave us the word 'gigot', as in 'gigot of lamb'?

3   Which part of the lamb *is* the 'gigot'?

4   Of which loch did the songwriter say 'I wish you were whisky'?

5   In the north-east of Scotland, if you were offered 'aleberry', would you expect a kind of porridge made with beer, a blackcurrant pudding or a cough mixture?

6   What is an Arbroath-pippin?

7   For which purpose would you use what's called an 'ashet' in Scots?

8   Can you name the important Scottish export in whose production people use nosing glasses?

9   What are the two main types of whisky bottled in Scotland?

10 A loganberry is a cross between a blackberry and which other fruit?

11 What kind of bread gave its name to a very posh way of speaking in Scotland?

12 If 'Kerr's' goes with 'Pinks', what goes with 'Golden'?

1   Unjumble these letters to find the name of an east-coast town: TERM SOON.

2   In the nursery rhyme, what is Wee Willie Winkie wearing as he 'rins through the toon'?

3   In which city could you see a show at the Royal Lyceum Theatre?

4   Which organisation is known as COSLA?

5   One of the main kinds of seal around our coast is the common seal. What is the other main kind?

6   Who owns the St Kilda group of islands? Is it the Ministry of Defence, the National Trust for Scotland or the Nature Conservancy Council?

7   What's the only Scottish daily newspaper without news stories on its front page?

8   What did King James VI describe as a custom 'lothsome to the eye, hatefull to the nose, harmefull to the braine'?

9   Which courts of the Church of Scotland are between the General Assembly and the presbyteries?

10 Immediately before he became Prime Minister, which government post did Lord Home hold?

11 Which motorway has a service area at Harthill?

12 How old do you have to be before you can bet in a betting shop in Scotland?

GAME 3

1   Did the Scots-born writer A.J. Cronin have the first name Andrew?

2   Does the line 'Hill you ho, boys; Let her go, boys' come from the 'Loch Tay Boat Song'?

3   Did Real Madrid play in the European Cup at Edinburgh in 1985?

4   Will you find Scotland's oldest university at St Andrews?

5   Did the Tay Road Bridge open in August 1965?

6   Did singer Lloyd Cole get to the top of the pop charts backed by a group called The Commotions?

7   Staying with pop, did disc jockey Tom Ferrie once sing with a group called The Riot Squad?

8   Are the headquarters of Renfrew District Council in Renfrew?

9   Is the town of Carnoustie further north than Coupar Angus?

10 Taking the normal AA recommended road route, is a trip from Aberdeen to Aberystwyth longer than a journey from Perth to Plymouth?

11 Is Barns Ness on the north coast of Scotland?

12 Can you visit the Angus Folk Museum at Glamis?

1   In spring of 1987, where would you have found a 'Male Stripper' and a 'Sonic Boom Boy'?

2   In which broadcast quiz is Ian Wallace a regular contestant with Denis Norden as his team mate?

3   Which instrument's music is traditionally divided into categories called 'small', 'middle' and 'great music'?

4   Who wrote the play of *Writer's Cramp*?

5   Which actress starred with Tom Conti in the 1986 film *Heavenly Pursuits*?

6   In which month of the year does the Edinburgh Festival begin?

7   What was the real first name of the writer Sir Compton Mackenzie?

8   Who was the famous daughter of a famous father who began to present the Breakfast Time television programme in autumn of 1986?

9   In the title of the song, which coin is 'crookit'?

10 In broadcasting, what kind of 'Radio' and 'Video' has included Gregor Fisher among its stars?

11 Can you name the television personality who was quoted saying he would 'never be welcome again' on Islay in 1985?

12 Which singer made famous the songs of 'A Gordon for Me' and 'The Northern Lights of Old Aberdeen'?

1   You'll see a bridge built by General Wade at this
    town on the River Tay (3 points).
    It has strong links with the Black Watch regiment (2
    points).
    And Robert Burns was inspired by the 'Birks' here
    (1 point).

2   This ruined royal castle stands in Argyll (3 points).
    It dates back to the thirteenth century and was held
    by Macdougalls and Campbells (2 points).
    And it is almost 4 miles north of Oban (1 point).

3   This island is popular with bird-lovers and is also
    known as Sheep Island (3 points).
    It was taken over by the National Trust for Scotland
    in 1954 (2 points).
    And it is famed for its knitwear (1 point).

4   This place has Three Sisters and the Chancellor as
    its neighbours to the north and south respectively (3
    points).
    It's a popular skiing centre (2 points).
    And it's linked with a sad historical event of 1692 (1
    point).

5   This town stands where the River Carron enters the
    Forth (3 points).
    It was our first deep-sea container port (2 points).
    And it's an important centre for the petro-chemical
    industry (1 point).

6   This was Scotland's fourth post-war new town,
    designated in 1962 (3 points).
    It has districts including Dedridge and Deans (2
    points).
    And it's close to the M8 motorway (1 point).

7   This west-coast town has a race-course (3 points).

Its Scottish League football team plays home matches at Somerset Park (2 points).
And it has strong Burns links (1 point).

8   This mountain has rather a misleading name (3 points).
It lies across the Dee Valley from the Cairngorm Range (2 points).
And Byron wrote a poem about it (1 point).

9   This loch is about 8 miles west of Callander, and 8 miles long (3 points).
You'll find Ellen's Isle in the loch (2 points).
And it has supplied water for the people of Glasgow (1 point).

10   This Lanarkshire town stands on the Powmillon Burn (3 points).
Avondale Castle is here (2 points).
And Lauder Ha', home of the entertainer Sir Harry Lauder, is nearby (1 point).

11   The 'Beltane Queen' is crowned in this town (3 points).
The Tweed joins the Eddleston Water here (2 points).
And Glentress Forest is nearby (1 point).

12   Youngsters go to school at the Nicholson Institute on this island (3 points).
A troop ship called the *Iolaire* sank near here on New Year's Day in 1919 with the loss of 200 men (2 points).
And the island is the home of BBC Radio nan Eilean (1 point).

1 Who was monarch when the Scottish and English Parliaments joined in 1707?

2 For work in which science did Sir William Ramsay win a Nobel Prize in 1904?

3 What's the name for the red deer breeding season that sounds like a track made by a wheel?

4 In which season of the year does this breeding take place in Scotland?

5 At the end of which loch does the village of Killin stand?

6 At a road crossing, what are the three colours on the disc of a lollipop lady's sign?

7 Which twentieth-century writer gave us books called *Glencoe*, *The High Girders*, and *The Highland Clearances*?

8 Cash from the ERDF sometimes comes to Scotland. What do these initials stand for?

9 Which Scottish political peer took the title 'of Marnock'?

10 In song, what colour of bonnets 'come over the Border'?

11 In which month is the quarter-day of Candlemas?

12 If Hallowe'en is on a Tuesday, on which day of the week does St Andrew's Day fall the same year?

1 In 1985, which decoration did Kenny Dalglish receive from the Queen?

2 Before becoming a sports broadcaster, what was Archie MacPherson's job? Was he a policeman, a bookmaker or a headmaster?

3 What's the name of Scotland's National Outdoor Training Centre near Aviemore, run by the Scottish Sports Council?

4 Who was rescued along with Eric Blunn off Cape Horn?

5 How did Selkirk football club make the national headlines on 8 December 1984?

6 In Scottish League football, what's the name of the 'Gable Endies'' home ground?

7 In the 1885 Scottish Cup, John Petrie of Arbroath set a record for the number of goals scored in a Scottish Cup match. How many did he net (to within two)?

8 In which month did the 1986 Commonwealth Games open in Scotland?

9 Were they the thirteenth, fourteenth or fifteenth?

10 At which ground did the 1988 Calcutta Cup international take place?

11 At the 1984 Olympics, in which sport did Alister Allan of Scotland win bronze?

12 Along with Mike McFarlane, who had a dead heat for gold in the men's 200 metres at the Brisbane Commonwealth Games?

GAME 3 SCOTS WORDS AND SAYINGS

1 Can you supply the missing word in this quotation from a song? 'These are my . . ., and this is my glen'?

2 At which occasion would you expect to see a 'strive' or a 'poor-oot'?

3 What kind of animal is a 'tup'?

4 Which bird has been known as the Ailsa cock, or the Ailsa parrot?

5 Who has been described as Auld Sooty, Auld Clootie and Auld Thrummy?

6 In poetry, which bird did James Hogg describe as 'bird of the wilderness, Blythesome and cumberless'?

7 What did 'reivers' do?

8 Was a 'cateran' a Highland reiver, a dagger, or a distant relative?

9 A 'hoggie' was a young . . . what?

10 In Scottish heraldry, which colour is 'gules'?

11 Still with Scottish heraldry, if a lion is 'gardant', how is it shown?

12 Are 'ferntickles' minnows, wild flowers or freckles?

1 If Moffat has toffee, which Borders town has 'snails'?

2 What delicacy are 'Eyemouth pales' – haddock or cheeses?

3 In Orkney, if you wanted 'fatty cutties', would you fish for them, bake them or dig for them?

4 In the song, if you're taking 'whisky on the Sunday', what's your tipple for the rest of the week?

5 Would you use a 'Scotch hand' when icing a cake, stirring a stew or handling butter?

6 In Shetland, what kind of fare is a 'buggle'?

7 What's usually the main ingredient of 'cock-a-leekie' soup?

8 Which creatures are farmed in Scotland and have varieties called 'brown' and 'rainbow'?

9 What type of cured fish are mainly linked with Loch Fyne?

10 What's the lowest percentage of fish that must legally be in fish cakes if you buy them in Scotland?

11 And to within 5 per cent, what's the smallest percentage of meat there must be in a cooked meat pie?

12 In Scotland, how old must a youngster be to enter a bar in a public house (apart from passing through the premises)?

1   Can you rearrange the letters in these words to form the name of a Tayside town: A FLY BREED?

2   Which of Scotland's Regions stretches furthest east?

3   What was the first name of the Labour leader, Keir Hardie?

4   Names of two district councils in Strathclyde begin with 'East'. What are their full names?

5   Which British national Sunday newspaper shares its name with Stirling's main local newspaper?

6   In geography, what are the 'Links of Forth' between Stirling and Alloa?

7   What did the Emperor Antoninus Pius order to be built in Scotland in the 140s AD?

8   Which royal burgh dating back to 1372 is now one of our new towns?

9   In which Region could you visit New Kelso – in Highland, Central, or Strathclyde?

10 How old must you be to serve on a jury in Scotland?

11 Which earl is the Lord High Constable of Scotland?

12 On which loch does the village of Arrochar stand?

GAME 4

1   Are the Tannahill Weavers best known for contemporary designs of tapestry?

2   If you drive the length of the A75 road, will you pass through Dumfries?

3   Still in Dumfries, was the King of Norway made a burgess of the town in 1962?

4   Is the Crawford Arts Centre in St Andrews?

5   In Scots, is the animal known as a 'gussie' a sheep?

6   Has Perth College of Further Education offered a course in rock music?

7   Was the Woman's Guild organisation founded by a minister's wife?

8   Is your hobby likely to be country dancing if you join the SCDA?

9   If you study at Tulliallan Castle, are you likely to be in the police?

10 In the football season 1987–88 did Second Division teams play fewer league matches than Premier Division clubs?

11 Would you go to the island of Barra to see Kisimul Castle?

12 If you dial the code 0224, are you phoning Dundee?

1 In which musical role is Bryden Thomson best known?

2 By which name did Moira King, born a civil engineer's daughter in Fife in 1926, come to be world famous?

3 In which industry did Kenneth McKellar begin his working career? Was it in electronics, printing or forestry?

4 What are the initials of the Reverend Jolly, as portrayed by Rikki Fulton?

5 Which is more popular in Scotland – going to the cinema, or attending football matches?

6 What do *Mr Bolfry* and *The Sleeping Clergyman* have in common with *Tobias and the Angel*?

7 Which Scottish show business personality became father of twins called Annabel and Robert in December 1985?

8 And if the daughter is Daisy and mum is Pamela, who's the well-known dad?

9 Which country dance has a name that also means the valley of the Spey?

10 What are the first names of the entertainers the Alexander Brothers?

11 Which present-day broadcaster came to fame as the folk-singing partner of Robin Hall?

12 Along with Des O'Connor, who took the 'Skye Boat Song' into the hit parade in 1986?

1 To which university post in Scotland was Winnie Mandela elected in 1987?

2 Still in 1987, where in Scotland did prison officers refuse for a time to admit prisoners?

3 In 1986, Breadalbane in Tayside was officially named as one of Scotland's first two 'environmentally sensitive areas'. What was the other area?

4 Bill McCue and Una McLean teamed up in two musical shows for Scottish Opera in 1986 – the first was *Annie*. What was the second show?

5 Which anniversary of its foundation was celebrated at Dumfries in 1986? Was it the town's 600th, 700th or 800th anniversary?

6 In the second half of the 1980s, MPs have been debating a 'community charge'. What is that charge designed to replace?

7 Which big industrial dispute of 1987 involved the NCU?

8 In Caithness, how did a fishbone find itself in the national headlines in summer of 1986?

9 In October 1986 Anne Miller and 'Rupert' were in the news. Who or what was 'Rupert', and why did they attract attention?

10 To which important post was Lord Sanderson appointed in the summer of 1987?

11 What was your job likely to have been if Mr John Pollock was your union's general secretary?

12 When he left the Scottish Office in 1986, which Cabinet post did Mr George Younger take over?

1 Which Glasgow road bridge has the same name as the capital of Jamaica?

2 Scott: in 'Waverley', which line follows 'My heart's in the Highlands, my heart is not here'?

3 On television, who is *Supercop*?

4 In which year was a surgeon called John Jamieson recorded as having brought the first umbrella to Glasgow? Was it in 1582, 1682 or 1782?

5 According to the song, which elderly relative is it impossible to remove forcibly from a form of public transport?

6 In which great church is the tomb of Prince Charles Edward Stuart?

7 To which song was a verse once added with the lines: 'May he sedition hush, And like a torrent rush, Rebellious Scots to crush'?

8 In the title of Molly Weir's book about her childhood in Glasgow, shoes were for which day of the week?

9 In song, which line follows: 'Come fill up my cup, come fill up my can'? And what's the song?

10 Three letters of the alphabet sound the same as Scottish rivers. Two points for two of them!

11 In song, of whom is it said that 'he's prood and he's great, His mind is ta'en up wi' the things o' the State'?

12 Collectively, how have Roy Williamson and Ronnie Browne usually been known on stage?

1   Going back to 1457, a decree from King James II said two sports should 'not be used' because their popularity was affecting archery practice needed to defend the realm. What were these two sports?

2   What was historic about the 1-1 draw in football between Scotland and England on 26 May 1984?

3   By which name is John Thomas Wilson, born in Kirkcaldy in March 1950, best known?

4   Which present-day international ground is the descendant of Raeburn Place, Hamilton Crescent and Inverleith?

5   The late Eric Liddell, Olympic athlete, was capped for Scotland in which other sport?

6   On 7 December 1980, two clubs from the same city contested the Scottish League Cup final. Who were they?

7   In which game would you expect to hear a cry of 'Soop! Soop!'?

8   Why did a Premier Division goal by Bobby Ford enter the record books one and a half minutes into a Dundee-Aberdeen match on 30 August 1975?

9   Which outdoor game, popular in Scotland, is played on a green that's bounded by a ditch and a bank?

10   In the Highlands, what's going on if the Lilywhites play the Can-Cans?

11   What does a 'Grouse and Orange' have in common with a 'Snipe and Purple' and a 'Teal and Red'?

12   Which Edinburgh park has the same name as a Glasgow football league club?

1 In Shetland dialect, what's the job of a 'flitman'?

2 Where on your body would you have worn 'gamashons'?

3 Which language gave us the word 'sporran'? Was it French, Danish or Gaelic?

4 Was a 'bonnet piece' a gold coin, an eagle's feather to adorn a hat, or a judge's wig?

5 How did that 'bonnet piece' get its name?

6 Scots mountains are sometimes given names to indicate how high they are. Which would be the smallest: a Munro, a Donald or a Corbett?

7 Where is Hecklebirnie?

8 If an Aberdonian told you it was about to 'bleeter', what kind of weather would you expect?

9 Which children's game has been known in Perthshire as 'blind-bole'?

10 What was your occupation if you were described as a 'blue gown' in Scotland?

11 In Angus, if you were a 'bruntie' were you a beggar, a blacksmith or a house-builder?

12 In days gone by, what was the job of a 'chapper up'?

GAME 4 FOOD AND DRINK

1 Which special day of the year was known in Scots as 'Fastern's E'en'?

2 In poetry, what is the 'Land o' Cakes'?

3 Which fruit grown in Scotland has varieties called Glen Clova, Glen Moy and Glen Prosen?

4 Which Scottish dish has the same name as sticky, lumpy snow in skiing?

5 What is a 'farl'?

6 What is a 'Finnan speldin'?

7 'Flannan' is Scots for 'flannel' but what have Aberdeenshire people named a 'flannan biscuit'?

8 Can you complete the saying: 'Like a hen on a het . . .'?

9 If you are like the hen in the saying, what sort of mood are you in?

10 Which confectionery has been known as a 'grannie's sooker'?

11 What are the main ingredients of a delicacy called 'skirlie'?

12 For which course of a meal would you eat 'Shivering Tam'?

1 Can you rearrange the letters in HOT GIN WILL to find the name of a Lothian town?

2 Which 'Wolf' had a stronghold at Garth Castle in Perthshire?

3 In alphabetical order, which of Scotland's universities comes last?

4 In the eighteenth century, who was Clementina Walkinshaw's famous sweetheart?

5 Which range of hills includes Dumyat and Ben Cleugh?

6 In which county is the most southerly point of the Scottish mainland?

7 Who wrote books called collectively the *Chronicles of the Canongate*?

8 What's the main airport in Scotland for scheduled flights that cross the Atlantic?

9 In which of our Firths are both the Mersehead Sands and the Blackshaw Bank?

10 How many of our Regions have names that include the name of a town?

11 And which Region has the same name as a Glasgow railway station?

12 How often was the reformer John Knox married – not at all, once, or twice?

GAME 5

GAME 5 YES OR NO?

1 Did Sir Walter Scott give the sub-title of 'A Tale of Flodden Field' to his poem 'Marmion'?

2 Was Sir Walter born at Sandyknowe in Tweeddale?

3 There are plenty of 'sikas' in Scotland. Are they a kind of spruce tree?

4 Is the RCCC the governing body of curling in Scotland?

5 Does the island of Gigha lie off the east side of the Mull of Kintyre?

6 Is the local radio station of Radio Tweed based at Hawick?

7 In Scots, is a 'steggie' a sharp pain in your back?

8 Would you expect to find a 'swilkie' in the sea?

9 Was it Dr Johnson who wrote: 'I have been trying all my life to like Scotchmen, and am obliged to desist from the experiment in despair'?

10 Are the headquarters of the Royal Highland and Agricultural Society of Scotland in Inverness?

11 Are the Rhinns of Kells hills in Kirkcudbrightshire?

12 If you're a pupil at Lochaber High School, do you study at Fort William?

1. The award-winning film of *Another Time, Another Place* came from a story by which Scottish writer?

2. Of which city is show business personality Andy Stewart a native?

3. In the chorus of which Scots song will you find the line: 'Yet a' the lads they smile at me'?

4. Which top children's cartoon family take their name from a Scottish loch?

5. In the title of the comic song made popular by June Imray, what did the 'quine' do at Inverurie?

6. Which distinguished series of radio lectures did the judge Lord McCluskey deliver in late 1986?

7. The film *Comfort and Joy* told of rivalry in Glasgow between what kind of firms?

8. In which year was Jim Diamond's chart-topping hit 'I Should Have Known Better' released?

9. In the 1987 film *The Name of the Rose*, who starred as a monk involved in a murder mystery?

10. Which Orkney-based composer became a knight in the New Year Honours of 1987?

11. What was the middle initial of Hugh Roberton, maestro of the Glasgow Orpheus Choir?

12. Which pop singer was supported by a group called 'The Luvvers'?

GAME 5 PLACE THE PLACE

1   It was called 'Clota' by Ptolemy (3 points).
It's 106 miles long (2 points).
And it became famed as a home of ship-building (1 point).

2   The Scottish Regalia were hidden from Cromwell's men in this castle (3 points).
It was a cruel east-coast prison for Covenanters (2 points).
And it's about 2 miles south of Stonehaven (1 point).

3   Lanimer Day is celebrated in summer in this county town (3 points).
You can go to the races here (2 points).
And it's said Wallace began his campaign for Scottish independence here (1 point).

4   There was once an observatory and an inn at this inaccessible spot (3 points).
There are several routes to get here on foot from Fort William (2 points).
And there's no higher place in Britain!(1 point).

5   A countess called Black Agnes defended a castle here 650 years ago (3 points).
This town was the scene of battles in 1296 and 1650 (2 points).
But now it's a pleasant Lothian holiday centre (1 point).

6   This is the home town of the poet Hugh MacDiarmid (3 points).
It stands on the Esk in Eskdale (2 points).
And it has an annual Border Riding ceremony (1 point).

7   The Argyllshire Gathering is held in this town each year (3 points).

Pulpit Hill is to the south (2 points).
And overlooking the town is the strange building,
McCaig's Folly (1 point).

8 This great structure was engineered by Sir John
Fowler in the 1880s (3 points).
You travel across it about 157 feet above water (2
points).
And the job of painting it gave the English language
a phrase for a never-ending task (1 point).

9 The name of this island town means 'King's haven'
(3 points).
It's 20 miles north-west of Kyle of Lochalsh (2
points).
And it's the capital of the 'Misty Isle' (1 point).

10 An eight-sided house built in memory of a
Dutchman once stood here (3 points).
Shells called 'Groatie buckies' are found on the
beach here (2 points).
And it is to the north as Land's End is to the south
(1 point).

11 This castle was once called Barrogil or Barragill (3
points).
It used to be a seat of the Earls of Caithness (2
points).
But it's now best-known as the Queen Mother's
northern home (1 point).

12 Here you can see some of the 8000 objects gathered
by one man in his lifetime (3 points).
You need to go to a country park in a city (2 points).
And into a treasure-house that's been specially built
for works of art (1 point).

1 What's the name of the lady who is supposed to have thrown a stool at the Bishop of Edinburgh in 1637?

2 In which century was the historic Declaration of Arbroath made?

3 In which language was the Declaration written?

4 What is the Loup of Fintry? Is it a waterfall, a glen or a cliff?

5 In which city could you study at the Robert Gordon's Institute of Technology?

6 During the week, what time can pubs usually open in Scotland (without getting an extension of hours)?

7 Which university has its astronomy department at Scotland's Royal Observatory?

8 In the shipping forecast, which sea area lies immediately due north of Malin?

9 If you land at Port Askaig, which island are you visiting?

10 With which town was Pulteneytown united at the beginning of the century?

11 Which islet formally became part of Scotland on 11 February 1972?

12 Who said of Scotland: 'Here I sit and governe it with my pen . . . which others could not do by the sword'?

1 Football: in which year did Celtic win the European Cup?

2 Which golf club hosted both the Scottish men's and women's amateur championships in 1987?

3 Because of snow in January 1987, which sporting international involving Scotland was postponed until April?

4 Three Scottish League football teams have points of the compass as part of their names. Can you name two of them?

5 In which sport have Chris Angel, Drew O'Neil and Harry Patterson been international stars for Scotland?

6 A 1986 book called *The Glory and the Dream* told the story of which football club?

7 Who opened the Commonwealth Games at Edinburgh in 1986?

8 After he left Pittodrie and Aberdeen Football Club in 1986, which ground became Alex Ferguson's new base?

9 In which year did Sandy Lyle win the Open golf championship in Britain?

10 In the 1986–7 season, Rangers and Dundee United competed in the same European football competition. Can you name it?

11 In which town can you go to a Scottish League football match at Bayview Ground?

12 In Scottish League football, who are the 'Diamonds'?

GAME 5 SCOTS WORDS AND SAYINGS

1 Where is the 'Athens of the north'?

2 What would you do with a 'squeeze-box'?

3 What was your occupation if you were nicknamed a 'grey breeks'?

4 What kind of prehistoric building is a 'broch'?

5 In the north-east of Scotland, what was the job of a 'browster'?

6 In Angus, did the phrase 'going off the carpet' mean: leaving home, getting married or losing a job?

7 What do you call the part of a bagpipe on which the melody is played?

8 If you're a 'red lichtie', what's your home town?

9 What is a 'tassie'?

10 Which language gave us the word 'tassie'?

11 If you 'claw someone's back', do you flatter them or spread false rumours about them?

12 Who or what is a 'clishmaclaver'? Is it a stick for stirring porridge, a gossip or a jenny wren?

GAME 5 FOOD AND DRINK

1 What kind of soup is 'bawd bree'?

2 Which tot of whisky sounds like a sixteenth of an ounce?

3 Who wrote the story of *Whisky Galore*?

4 In *Whisky Galore*, what was the name of the island whose natives claimed the precious liquid from the shipwreck?

5 Which Scottish product comes in varieties including light, heavy, special and export?

6 What is defined in the dictionary as 'a kind of pudding usually made by slowly stirring oatmeal in boiling water'?

7 Which city was said to be famous for 'jute, jam and journalism'?

8 In song, who 'brew'd a peck o' maut'?

9 If you were offered a Nithsdale pint of milk last century, would you have expected less, the same or more than the standard Scots pint?

10 In the song of 'Caller Herrin'', from which river were the fish 'new drawn'?

11 If you ate a 'buckie', would you be tasting a scone, a shellfish or a blaeberry?

12 In England, what name is given to the blaeberry?

1 The name of an Ayrshire village is concealed in these jumbled-up letters: MADE SIN. Which village?

2 Who was the famous tenant of Mossgiel Farm around 200 years ago?

3 In *Who's Who*, which MP has listed his recreations as being 'blunt and sharp at the same time' and also 'the cure and eradication of British tick fever'?

4 Which industry has a shop window at the 'Offshore Europe' exhibition when it's in Scotland?

5 If you sailed due south from the mainland at Scotland's most easterly point, would you land on the shores of France, Belgium or England?

6 And if you flew due east from Lerwick, over which country would you fly next?

7 What is King Edward VII said to have described as 'a Highland barn with a thousand draughts'?

8 What's unusual about the location of the Dean Village?

9 Which famous engineering project stands partly on the Mackintosh Rock?

10 Which member of the Royal family is Colonel in Chief of the Black Watch?

11 How many rooms were there in a cottage called a 'but and ben'?

12 In which city could you study at the Kingsway Technical College?

GAME 6

GAME 6 YES OR NO?

1   Is the popular garden shrub, the forsythia, named after a Scottish gardener?

2   On the Clyde, is Glasgow's Victoria Bridge upstream from the Albert Bridge?

3   Was it King James II who came to the throne of Scotland in 1437?

4   Is there a kind of rock called Ben Moreite after Ben More on Mull?

5   Does Radio Scotland broadcaster Neville Garden play the bassoon in his spare time?

6   Is Prince Charles the Colonel in Chief of the Gordon Highlanders?

7   In Scots, does the word 'wally' mean 'excellent'?

8   Is Garroch Head the most southerly point of the Isle of Arran?

9   Will you find the village of Crannachan in Highland Region?

10 Does the Moderator of the General Assembly of the Church of Scotland normally serve for one year?

11 Is your 'wizzen' a part of your throat?

12 Have Lammas Fairs in Scotland traditionally been held in autumn?

GAME 6 ENTERTAINMENT

1   Who was the Scottish singer who took 'Holy City' into the top fifty in 1969?

2   Television: in *All Creatures Great and Small*, who plays the young vet Calum Buchanan?

3   In Scottish song, which island does the chorus praise: 'O my own one, O my Isle; O my dear, my native Isle'?

4   Television: in the comedy series *City Lights*, what's the first name of Willie Melvin's girlfriend?

5   Down television's memory lane, what was the first name of the housekeeper played by Barbara Mullen in *Dr Finlay's Casebook*?

6   In song, what robbed Jock of 'the wee bit sense he had'?

7   In a catchphrase, who says things are 'Fandabi-dozy'?

8   In which year did television officially come to Scotland? Was it 1950, 1951 or 1952?

9   In which television series is Carole Baxter one of the two stars?

10 In the film *Heavenly Pursuits*, what was the occupation of Tom Conti?

11 In which Scottish city was that film set?

12 On radio, who is 'your naughty, dotty Scottie'?

1   In May 1985 people from many parts of the world came to a 'Hamefarin'' festival to renew links with which part of Scotland?

2   Which Scottish nuclear power station was the subject of a public inquiry in 1986 over a planned reprocessing plant there?

3   Which foreign country did the 1985 Edinburgh Festival take as its special theme?

4   In the mid-1980s, what was the name given to the periodic change in the system that affected rates throughout Scotland?

5   What was the subject of James Grassie's 1983 book *Highland Experiment*?

6   In November 1985, what unusual development occurred to do with second-class letter post?

7   Which politician published a book in the 1980s about his *Border Country*?

8   In 1985, which Scottish city was ordered to cut its rates by a special parliamentary order?

9   Who resigned as MP for the Western Isles in 1987?

10 A romance between Sam Sam and Naomi in Edinburgh was in the news in the summer of 1985. Who were the romantic pair?

11 What four bonuses did the dry summer of 1984 give the Royal Commission on Ancient and Historical Monuments?

12 Studies by the Fraser of Allander Institute at Strathclyde University are often in the news. What is the subject of these studies?

1   What's the title, if the second line of the song is 'Oh, Mist rolling in from the sea'?

2   In Scotland, who can marry two people on the same day?

3   If you enjoy Strawberry Switchblade, do you like creamy desserts, pop music, or gardening?

4   In which Region is the town of Sanquhar?

5   What is described formally as 'a saltire argent in a field azure'?

6   It's between 25 and 43 miles wide, and it lies between the Outer Hebrides, Ross and Cromarty and Sutherland. What is it called?

7   If you walk out into Gordon Street, at which main Glasgow railway station have you just arrived?

8   Which town has had Allen Adams and Norman Buchan as its MPs?

9   Which town is 'home' to a local newspaper called the *Buchan Observer*?

10 Which canal crosses the Northern Kintyre peninsula?

11 According to the title of the children's song by Matt McGinn, what colour was that yo-yo?

12 If people are members of the SWRI, where would you expect them to be living?

GAME 6 SPORTS

1   For which distance did Liz Lynch win gold for Scotland in the 1986 Commonwealth Games?

2   In which sport has a young star called Stephen Hendry made his name in recent years?

3   Which Scottish sport is the closest relation to Ireland's game of hurling?

4   In which year did Aberdeen win football's European Cup-Winners' Cup at Gothenburg?

5   When Scotland's footballers travelled to Mexico in 1986, for how many successive World Cup final stages had we qualified?

6   Which sport made Peter Keenan famous in the 1940s and 1950s?

7   In the Scottish FA Cup Final of 1986, which team lost to Aberdeen?

8   In 1983, which top sports job did Michael Bonallack take up in Scotland?

9   In which activity has Martin Bell made his name by going down from the top?

10 Football: which year saw the Centenary Final of the Scottish Cup?

11 In December 1986 Copenhagen hosted the European championships of which popular Scottish sport?

12 Which football team knocked Rangers out of the Scottish Cup in January 1987?

GAME 6 SCOTS WORDS AND SAYINGS

1 What kind of headgear, sometimes known as a 'cockit bonnet', has the same name as an Inverness-shire glen?

2 What was a 'corn kist' used for?

3 What sort of mood are you in if you're 'crabbit'?

4 In the north and east of Scotland, which part of your body is the 'crannie'?

5 On the island of Arran, is 'The String' a river, a road or a hill?

6 In the home, what was a 'cruisie' used for?

7 Which common flower was known in Scots as the 'cuckoo-hood'?

8 Which game would you play with what is called a 'dambrod' in Scots?

9 What time is the 'e'e of the morn'?

10 If you had a sore 'elbuck', which part of your body would be in discomfort?

11 Place names: as in Kilmarnock or Kildonan, what does the prefix 'Kil' mean?

12 What kind of bird is a 'hoodie'?

GAME 6 FOOD AND DRINK

1 If you moved to a new house, someone might have wished you luck by saying: 'May the mouse ne'er leave your girnel wi' the tear-drop in its e'e'. What is a 'girnel'?

2 Which part of a sheep goes to make the traditional broth called 'Powsowdie'?

3 What was a 'bannock stane'?

4 What do you do if you take a 'willie waught'?

5 How many 'fardells' would you expect to get from a round cake?

6 If you were served a 'Glasgow bailie', what would be on your plate?

7 What are the main ingredients of Edinburgh rock?

8 What are caboc, hramsa and Dunlop all examples of?

9 What's the standard English phrase for the Scots 'as plain as parritch'?

10 If Atholl is linked with brose, what goes with Abernethy?

11 Can you complete this Burns quotation? 'Go fetch to me a pint o' wine; An' fill it in a . . .'

12 From which adventure classic by a Scottish writer does this quotation come: 'Many's the long night I've dreamed of cheese – toasted, mostly'?

GAME 6 GENERAL KNOWLEDGE (2)

1   Can you find the name of a west coast island by rearranging the letters in the word: LIES?

2   In which town are the headquarters of the Scottish Examination Board – Perth, Paisley or Dalkeith?

3   Of whom or of what did Robert Louis Stevenson write that he loved 'with all my heart. She gives me cream with all her might, To eat with apple tart'?

4   Under the Treaty of Perth, Norway gave the Western Isles to Scotland along with which island?

5   What's the Canadian Province whose name means 'New Scotland'?

6   What was the first name of the Mr MacMillan who pioneered the bicycle in 1839?

7   Which cloth is particularly linked with Harris in Scotland and Donegal in Ireland?

8   Why do we remember Alexander 'Greek' Thomson?

9   What famous line did the Ninety-third Sutherland Highlanders form in 1854?

10 In which war did that 'line' make its celebrated stand?

11 Which Scottish university has its headquarters at Regent Walk?

12 Which Scottish county includes the name of an English town?

GAME 7

GAME 7 YES OR NO?

1 Is the Tay Road Bridge to the east of the Tay Rail Bridge?

2 Was the graphophone an early version of the gramophone invented by Alexander Graham Bell?

3 Can you go to a show at the Brunton Theatre in Kirkcaldy?

4 Is the Scots fir tree another name for the Scots pine?

5 Was the explorer Mungo Park a native of Lanarkshire?

6 Is there a kind of fish called the Mungo-Park?

7 Does Garve Island lie off the north coast of Scotland?

8 Is the Royal Scottish Academy of Music and Drama based in Edinburgh?

9 Was the inventor of the bicycle a blacksmith by trade?

10 Was the 'father of radar' a native of Brechin?

11 Did the poet Hugh MacDiarmid publish *Hymns to Lenin* in the 1930s?

12 Is Borders Region smaller in area than Central Region?

1   Besides being a well-known singer, what other job is Peter Morrison qualified to do?

2   Which actor played Andy, in television's *EastEnders* series?

3   Who was the Scottish actress who was *My Wife Next Door*?

4   Who was the Scots star of the 1986 film *Highlander*?

5   In the television series *Porridge*, who played the prison officer who was in a constant battle of wits with Ronnie Barker?

6   How many 'Estates' are there in the title of the satirical play by Sir David Lindsay?

7   Which 1985 film told the story of two twentieth-century Scottish 'outlaws' who made touring buses their prey?

8   Which rock band played the soundtrack music of that film?

9   Who wrote the poetic play of 1725 called *The Gentle Shepherd*?

10   Which folk-singing act shares a name with what the dictionary calls 'semi-circular mountain recesses'?

11   Which Glasgow theatre do you link with 119 Gorbals Street?

12   Which of these J.M. Barrie characters was created first – Peter Pan or the Admirable Crichton?

1   This castle was built between 1679 and 1691 on an
    old Douglas stronghold (3 points).
    There's a seventeenth-century solid silver chandelier
    here which weighs 9 stone (2 points).
    It's near Thornhill and is a seat of the Dukes of
    Buccleuch (1 point).

2   This Argyll town was once known as Kilkerran (3
    points).
    It's situated on a loch, which has Davaar Island at its
    entrance (2 points).
    Machrihanish airport lies to the west (1 point).

3   This Borders abbey was founded in the twelfth
    century (3 points).
    It stands near the Tweed, and was badly damaged
    several times by English soldiers (2 points).
    It's the burial place of Sir Walter Scott and Field
    Marshal Earl Haig (1 point).

4   This village on the Caledonian Canal was called after
    the middle name of the Duke of Cumberland (3
    points).
    Cherry Island is just to the north, in Loch Ness (2
    points).
    And General Wade built a fort here (1 point).

5   Many kings are buried on this small island (3
    points).
    You can sail to it by ferry from Fionnphort on Mull
    (2 points).
    It's been celebrated for its links with Christianity
    since St Columba came here over 1400 years ago (1
    point).

6   Cardinal Beaton was murdered here in 1546 (3
    points).

It's the home of Scotland's oldest university (2 points).
And it is also famous as the base of the 'Royal and Ancient' Golf Club (1 point).

7   This castle overlooks the Tweed and dates back to 1721 (3 points).
It was built by William Adam, and Playfair added to it (2 points).
It's the home of the Duke of Roxburghe (1 point).

8   This island town stands on Bressay Sound (3 points).
There's an annual fire festival here each January (2 points).
And it's the 'capital' of its island group (1 point).

9   It's on top of Abbey Craig (3 points).
It's a landmark in the Stirling area (2 points).
And it's a memorial to a great Scottish patriot (1 point).

10 This famous home was built on the site of a farm once called 'Clarty Hole' (3 points).
There are strong literary connections (2 points).
And it's beside the River Tweed, near Melrose (1 point).

11 This town was once the home of the Arctic explorer Sir John Ross (3 points).
It stands at the head of Loch Ryan (2 points).
And there's a short sea crossing to Northern Ireland from here (1 point).

12 A Victorian called Osgood MacKenzie, helped by the Gulf Stream, takes credit for the existence of this tourist attraction (3 points).
A promontory in Ross and Cromarty is the scene (2 points).
And sub-tropical plants flourish here in the same latitude as Siberia (1 point).

1 In which Region are the Sidlaw Hills?

2 Unless signs say otherwise, what's the maximum speed limit for a car on an ordinary dual carriageway?

3 In the absence of signs to the contrary, what's the speed limit for your car on a single carriageway?

4 What's the title of the Crown's chief law officer for Scotland?

5 With which country did Scotland have the 'Auld Alliance'?

6 Which of these towns is furthest north – Inverness, Nairn or Kyle of Lochalsh?

7 Which garden flower was named after the victor of the Battle of Culloden?

8 In which Scottish Firth is the oil terminal of Hound Point?

9 Which great writer was born at Ecclefechan in 1795?

10 Ruined castles at Kirkcaldy and near Peterhead carry the same name as a big industrial complex in Lanarkshire. What is that name?

11 Which story by Sir Walter Scott, published in 1816, has the nickname of a certain Robert Paterson as its title?

12 Which city is the setting for the 1950s book *Dancing In the Streets*?

1 Of which London football club did George Graham become manager in May 1986?

2 What do the names of the Scottish League football clubs of Alloa, Forfar and Dunfermline all have in common?

3 What kind of racing came to an end at Shawfield Stadium on 25 October 1986?

4 Which special event of 1986 was commemorated by a specially minted £2 coin?

5 Which Scottish sportsmen sound like clips used to make hair look prettier?

6 Which sport was featured on the special 17-pence Commonwealth Games stamp of 1986?

7 If you 'turn the cat' in Scots, which athletic feat do you perform?

8 Who was the newspaper proprietor who tried to improve the finances of the 1986 Commonwealth Games?

9 In which sport has Cathy Panton made her name?

10 Which Scottish League football club was relegated in both 1984 and 1985?

11 In July 1985, which athlete's appearance led to a row over banners at Meadowbank Stadium?

12 In 1985, what did the Popplewell inquiry recommend that English football fans should carry, but Scots fans needn't?

GAME 7 SCOTS WORDS AND SAYINGS

1 Can you complete the name of the children's kissing game that begins 'Bee baw . . .'?

2 In the Scottish saying, if you go to 'the black gate', what's happening to you?

3 Which illegal activity was once known as the 'gentle traffic' in Scotland?

4 What relation to you is your 'guid billie'?

5 Which bird is a 'houlet'?

6 And which bird is the 'mavis'?

7 Which county was once called Edinburghshire?

8 What's the biggest town on the so-called 'Long Island'?

9 If you sell a house in Scotland, for what purpose would you need a document called a 'disposition'?

10 Can you think of an English proverb that's the opposite of the Scottish 'Lang leal, lang puir'?

11 And which English proverb means the same as 'Ill comes on war's back'?

12 Place names: what does 'wick' mean, as in the names of Lerwick, and Wick in Caithness?

1 Which was the larger of these old measures – a mutchkin or a choppin?

2 When would you drink a 'deoch an' doris'?

3 'Garvies' were once a rich export trade to Scandinavia for the fishermen of Bo'ness. What were they?

4 Who called a volume of his autobiography *Salt In My Porridge*?

5 What kind of soup is Cullen Skink?

6 Would you have expected mussels in Musselburgh Pie?

7 For which course of a meal would you serve Edinburgh Fog?

8 Would you eat a 'tappit hen'?

9 Who's the comic cartoon character with a taste for 'cow pie'?

10 In Burns' 'Address to a Haggis', what line follows: 'Fair fa' your honest, sonsie face'?

11 Can you fill in the blanks with the first names of these three well-known Scottish food writers: ——— McNeill, —— Baxter and ——— Craig?

12 According to the proverb, what do you need to 'sup with a Fifer'?

1 Rearrange the letters of the words NEAR THRUST – and you'll find the name of a Fife coast town!

2 Which of the armed services has an important base at Leuchars in Fife?

3 Which Fife village shares its name with a famous musical work by Handel?

4 Which is higher – the Bass Rock or Dumbarton Rock?

5 Which two local government Regions of Scotland share the same police force?

6 In the Borders Common Riding ceremonies, if Duns has a Reiver, who does Kelso have?

7 Which earl was known in history as 'Archibald Bell-the-Cat'?

8 In story, what was the type of boat sailed by Para Handy?

9 Which Aberdeenshire village sounds like 2.54 centimetres?

10 Who was the father of King James VII?

11 To which creature did Burns dedicate a poem 'on seeing one on a lady's bonnet at church'?

12 By tradition, how did the Duchess of Gordon help recruitment to the Gordon Highlanders regiment almost 200 years ago?

GAME 8

1   Did General Wolfe, of Quebec fame, also fight at Culloden?

2   In Scotland, does compulsory schooling begin at five and end at sixteen?

3   Will you read columnist Barbara Bruce in the *Sunday Mail*?

4   Was Alistair MacLean the author of the thriller *Where Eagles Dare*?

5   Is the town of Peebles in Tweeddale District?

6   Does Lord Todd of Trumpington hold the post of Chancellor of Glasgow University?

7   Is comedian Andy Cameron a native of Glasgow?

8   Is newscaster Sir Alastair Burnet a native of Edinburgh?

9   Is Ben Lawers in Tayside higher than Snowdon?

10 In Scottish schools, are there more men teachers than women teachers?

11 When she made her first radio broadcast, was singer Moira Anderson just four years old?

12 Does the village of Ecclefechan lie to the west of Dumfries?

GAME 8 ENTERTAINMENT

1 Which Scottish television personality was elected Rector of Edinburgh University in March 1985?

2 Hamish MacCunn was born in Greenock in 1868. He is best remembered for his gifts in which of the arts?

3 In which stage show did Lulu star in 1987 and 1988 along with George Cole?

4 Which Scottish country dance band leader is known for his singing as well as playing – with songs like 'The Lights of Lochindaal' and 'Happy Birthday'?

5 With which musical instrument is that band leader usually linked?

6 What does Rachel Rae have in common with Mrs McLeod and Kate Dalrymple?

7 What are the surnames of folk music duo Cilla and Artie?

8 Which Scot became famous for his songs 'Two Lovely Black Eyes' and 'The Man who Broke the Bank at Monte Carlo'?

9 Which playwright gave us *The Other Dear Charmer*?

10 What name was given to the music, defined in the dictionary as 'a jazz type of folk music', which Lonnie Donegan helped to make popular in the 1950s?

11 Which Scottish comedian had the catch-phrase 'Clairty, clairty'?

12 And which great Scottish professional funny man was born David Williams in 1895?

GAME 8 NEWS OF THE '80s

1 Mr Albert Wheeler was in the news in 1984 and early 1985 – in which job?

2 He visited Scotland in December 1985 with his wife Raisa, and now he's one of the most powerful men in the world. Who is he?

3 What was the Tour de Trossachs, held in October 1985?

4 What's the date on pound coins which show a Scottish thistle?

5 What did England stop issuing at the end of 1984, that we still produce in Scotland?

6 Which BBC orchestra had its fiftieth birthday on 3 December 1985?

7 In the mid-1980s, where did the new Scottish Exhibition Centre open?

8 Who officially opened it?

9 A new form of transport came to Scotland in the 1980s – the C5. How many wheels did it have on the road?

10 Who is the Shadow Scottish Secretary?

11 Which former political party leader did Mr Jim Wallace succeed as an MP in 1983?

12 Which Scots-born multi-millionaire had a British Rail loco named after him in 1985, the 150th anniversary of his birth?

1 If you dial 0738, which city are you phoning?

2 In the 1960s in Scotland, what did the Poor Souls have especially in common with the Poets and the Beatstalkers?

3 On which loch does Fort William stand?

4 Which Scottish engineer had a new town, 20 miles north-west of Birmingham, named after him in 1963?

5 Where in Scotland can you see concrete 'Churchill Barriers'?

6 Which regiment is nicknamed 'Pontius Pilate's Bodyguard'?

7 What's the number of the motorway which bypasses Stirling?

8 How many Scottish Regions share a border with Dumfries and Galloway Region?

9 On which island can you see Lochranza Castle?

10 Which island of the Inner Hebrides has a name which is the same as a Scots word for a headland?

11 Which town is 'home' to the Scottish College of Textiles?

12 Which place is missing from this group: Dunnet Head, Mull of Galloway and Buchan Ness?

1   At which arena did boxer Jim Watt win four of his six world title fights?

2   In which month is the 'Glorious Twelfth'?

3   Where in Scotland were the world junior curling championships played in March 1985?

4   In which year did 'Ally's Tartan Army' go to Argentina, and why?

5   Of which Scottish football club is Wallace Mercer the chairman?

6   How did a prize of sweets for a race put a ten-year-old Montrose boy into the headlines in 1985?

7   In Scottish League football, what would be the difference in points between a team that won four matches and drew six, and another team that won six and drew four?

8   An empty bus was boarded by a football team, a shinty side and a rugby union team. If there were fifty-four passenger seats on the bus, how many would be empty if all the sportsmen were on board?

9   In which sport, run in Scotland by the STA, do you have competition routines of ten 'bounces'?

10   When would you have used a 'cairn net'? Would it be when fishing, climbing or playing hockey?

11   In Scottish League football, which Tayside club has the word 'City' in its name?

12   In August 1985, which golf title did Howard Clark win after a play-off with Sandy Lyle?

1 Which city is sometimes described as 'east windy, west endy'?

2 Which Fife town has been nicknamed 'the Lang Toon'?

3 In standard English, what is a 'lum hat'?

4 Which creature is known as the 'bauckie bird' in Scots?

5 Why is that a misleading name?

6 In Scotland, which creature is sometimes called the 'sweet marten'?

7 Can you identify the creatures found in Scotland, of which Kenneth McKellar has sung that 'Wi' teeth like piranhas, They drive you bananas'?

8 In geography, what is a 'law' in Scotland?

9 Which shrub is the 'laylock'?

10 Which sport is 'the lead-stanes' in Scots?

11 Which weapon was named after Lochaber?

12 In days gone by, why didn't children care too much for a 'black Lochgelly'?

1 Norway lobsters are an important catch for our fishermen. But what are they better known as, on the menu?

2 What's the first line of Burns' 'Selkirk Grace'?

3 In the ballad, where did the king sit 'drinking the blude-red wine'?

4 In Scotland, it's 'minced collops'. What would it be in England?

5 Besides milk, what are the main ingredients of 'Auld Man's Milk'?

6 In England, they're often known as drop scones. What do we call them?

7 Is 'feather fowlie' a soup, a stew or a dessert?

8 According to Dr Johnson, what was generally given to horses in England, 'but in Scotland supports the people'?

9 If you were offered 'stoorum', would you expect to drink it or eat it?

10 Which Scottish town is the home of pastry 'bridies'?

11 Traditionally, which meat is used in 'Scotch pies'?

12 What's the main ingredient of Partan Bree soup?

1 Unscramble these letters – SHIELD ALL – to spell the name of a Lanarkshire village.

2 What's unusual about the name of Glenelg in Inverness-shire?

3 In which of the arts did Anne Redpath and Robin Philipson become best known this century?

4 What kind of business has trade bodies called the SMMT and the SMTA?

5 In place names, which two words go before: Earn, Orchy, Allan and Weir?

6 How many of the Queen's children were educated at Gordonstoun?

7 Which part of your body has the same name as a loch stretching 17 miles to the north-west of Lairg?

8 Which Scottish Saint was canonised in October 1976 at St Peter's in Rome?

9 Which famous pirate, who was executed in 1701, was born at Greenock?

10 What were named the Seven Sisters of Borthwick? Were they guns, hills or coastal rocks?

11 Which local government Region is also known as a Kingdom?

12 Which animal found in Scotland is known formally as 'mustela erminea'?

GAME 9

1   Is Glasgow further west than Madrid?

2   In 1986, did Glasgow Cathedral celebrate its 800th anniversary?

3   Was Darnley the third husband of Mary Queen of Scots?

4   Is it true that only one out of ten of the Scottish population takes part in an outdoor sports activity?

5   Did John Logie Baird give his first public showing of television in the same year as the General Strike?

6   If you order Scotch woodcock from a menu, should you expect a dish of scrambled eggs and anchovies?

7   In a civil case in the sheriff court, are there twelve members of the jury?

8   Is the highest value of a Scottish bank note £100?

9   Is the Highland Region larger in area than Wales?

10 Mountains: is the 'Cobbler' higher than Ben Arthur?

11 Scott facetiously called a certain everyday object a 'monotroch'. Would you expect to use a 'monotroch' in the kitchen?

12 When a body called the International Mire Conservation Group met in Scotland in 1986, did they discuss peat bogs?

GAME 9 ENTERTAINMENT

1 Which 'Gordon' was 'Hudson' in the servants' hall?

2 Which great Scottish actor gave George Cole his first big chance on stage, in 1940?

3 In the British Academy awards for 1983, announced in 1984, who won the award for Best Newcomer?

4 In which film?

5 Which leading Scots-born actor and director had West End stage appearances that included *They're Playing Our Song* in 1980 and *Romantic Comedy* in 1983?

6 Which comedian uses the catch-phrase 'See You, Jimmy?' in his comic role as a Scot?

7 Which national event was supported by a Royal Gala variety show in Edinburgh in the summer of 1985?

8 Which Ultravox pop star was co-founder with Bob Geldof of the Band-Aid famine relief project?

9 Which comedian had a golf tournament at Edinburgh named after him in September 1985?

10 Which nautical cartoon captain was created by John Ryan, born in Edinburgh in 1921?

11 If Sydney Devine is your favourite singer, which type of music is to your taste?

12 Which Scottish entertainer made banana-shaped wellies famous?

GAME 9 PLACE THE PLACE

1   The song 'Scots Wha Ha'e' is said to have been
    written by Burns in this small town (3 points).
    About half a mile to the north is the site of a
    Galloway Roman fort (2 points).
    And the layout of the town has been likened to the
    New Town of Edinburgh (1 point).

2   Lord Clyde, Prince Albert, William Gladstone and
    Robert Burns are all to be found here (3 points).
    It's a square in the heart of a city (2 points).
    And in 1888 Queen Victoria came here to open a
    richly-styled City Chambers (1 point).

3   The Boar of Badenoch and the Sow of Atholl are to
    be seen from the top of this pass (3 points).
    The public rail network in Britain reaches its highest
    point at the summit of the pass (2 points).
    And to see it by road you drive along the A9 (1
    point).

4   This island is sometimes called the 'Garden of the
    Hebrides' (3 points).
    Magnetic rock in its Compass Hill is said to affect
    ships' compasses (2 points).
    And the island is 3 miles north-west of Rhum (1
    point).

5   Once a fishing village called Newark, it was here
    that the main Clyde customs house was built in 1710
    (3 points).
    The pioneering boat the 'Comet' was built here (2
    points).
    And this was Glasgow's harbour till the Clyde was
    deepened (1 point).

6   This town was 'home' to film star Deborah Kerr and
    to television pioneer John Logie Baird (3 points).

It is named after the wife of Sir James Colquhoun of Luss, who laid out part of the town (2 points).
And it stands at the entrance to Gare Loch (1 point).

7   This Borders home is claimed to be Scotland's oldest continuously inhabited house (3 points).
Its own beer is produced at a small brewhouse (2 points).
And gates flanked by stone bears will stay shut till a Stuart regains the throne (1 point).

8   This royal event traditionally takes place on the first Saturday of September (3 points).
Strength and speed are put to the test (2 points).
And the scene is a village near where the Clunie and Dee meet (1 point).

9   George Orwell wrote *1984* on this island (3 points).
The whirlpool of Corrievreckan lies to the north (2 points).
And Craighouse is the island's only village (1 point).

10 Once, this northern town was Scotland's main port for trade with Scandinavia (3 points).
To the west is Pennyland Farm, birthplace of Sir William Smith, founder of the Boys' Brigade (2 points).
The Dounreay atomic energy establishment is 7 miles away (1 point).

11 Prime Minister Ramsay MacDonald was born at No. 1 Gregory Place in this town (3 points).
An air base is nearby (2 points).
And the town is 5 miles north of Elgin (1 point).

12 This landmark is to be seen where a burn drops 200 feet from Loch Skeen (3 points).
Its name sounds as though it's part of a horse (2 points).
And it's about 10 miles north-east of Moffat (1 point).

GAME 9 GENERAL KNOWLEDGE (1)

1   If capes go with Inverness, which items of apparel should you link with Paisley?

2   After which King George is Glasgow's George Square named?

3   What kind of animal is a 'blackface'?

4   Which important industry has formed a group called the United Kingdom Offshore Operators' Association?

5   In Scottish place names, which single word goes before each of these: George, Matilda, Augustus and William?

6   In the 1960s, which university was formed from a college of St Andrews University?

7   In which island group is our most northerly whisky distillery to be found?

8   Who's the sister of the Earl of St Andrews?

9   How many Districts in Scotland have Lord Provosts?

10 Who wrote: 'The cruellest lies are often told in silence'? Was it Carlyle, Scott or Stevenson?

11 Which top tourist attraction of the present day was built 200 years ago for the Earl of Cassillis in Ayrshire?

12 Which Scottish duke is also the Duke of Chatelherault in France?

1 Which British championships were contested at Murrayfield in Edinburgh in August 1985? Were they for figure skating, five-a-side rugby or chess?

2 Which top sporting job in Scotland is done by Mr Jim Farry?

3 Who was the Scottish athlete who won the 800 metres at the Europa Cup meeting in Moscow in 1985?

4 What's the captain of a curling team called?

5 In which sport, followed in Scotland, do you watch a variometer and train for 'bronze C', 'silver C' and 'gold C' badges?

6 Why did newspapers and broadcasters talk about 'Freuchie fever' in September 1985?

7 Which sport is usually associated with Muirfield, near Gullane?

8 Which country park is one of Scotland's main rowing venues?

9 On a shinty pitch, what is the 'hail'?

10 Which Scottish League football club had its story told in a 1985 book called *Rags to Riches*?

11 In which sport did Derrick Grant from Hawick become Scotland's national coach in 1985?

12 Which Scottish League football club has a ground with the same name as the 'capital' of the Isle of Man?

GAME 9 SCOTS WORDS AND SAYINGS

1   Give a reason for your answer to this question, please. Would you have cared to sample a 'Lockerbie lick'?

2   If you are described as a 'man o' mony morns', are you somebody who delays action, an old man or a church minister?

3   Which animal has been known as a 'mappie' in Scotland?

4   What's the word for a festival of Gaelic music and literature that originally meant a council or parliament?

5   What's the usual name for the bird known as the 'wood grouse'?

6   In history, what was made up by the 'Three Estates' in Scotland?

7   What's the name given to the speech in praise of Robert Burns, given at Burns Suppers?

8   In 1639, what was the 'Trot of Turriff'? Was it an illness, a battle or a barn dance?

9   What is a 'neep cleek'? Is it a tool for harvesting turnips or a golf club?

10 Which fictitious person is called 'Nip-nebs' in Scotland?

11 Would you eat the Clean Pease Strae, dance it or wear it?

12 In Scots, what kind of news was 'piper's news'?

GAME 9 FOOD AND DRINK

1 Which fruit has varieties called Ben Lomond and Ben More?

2 What would you have kept in a 'gardyveen'?

3 At which Tayside town are the headquarters of the Government's Freshwater Fisheries Laboratory to be found?

4 What were 'Culross girdles' made of?

5 Which food begins as 'fry' and grows through stages called 'parr', 'smolts' and 'grilse'?

6 Which song about confectionery has a chorus that begins: 'Ally, bally, ally bally bee'?

7 Which part of a meal took place at the 'jawbox'?

8 Which part of Scotland became known for local sweeties called 'Soor Plooms'?

9 What colour are 'Soor Plooms'?

10 At which annual festival would you expect to taste treacle-spread scones which are hung on a string?

11 What's the singular of 'scampi'?

12 What becomes Scotch if you surround it with sausage-meat?

GAME 9 GENERAL KNOWLEDGE (2)

1   Hidden in the words THE RED PEA is a
    north-eastern town. What's its name?

2   What's the longest jail sentence that a Sheriff can
    impose in Scotland?

3   In the title of the Harry Lauder song, where was he
    'roaming'?

4   Which farm horse shares its name with a district of
    Strathclyde?

5   History: what was the first name of the ill-fated
    'Maid of Norway'?

6   In a parliamentary election, a constituency returns
    an MP. In a district council election, what's the
    name for the area that returns a councillor?

7   Can you be elected to both a regional and a district
    council?

8   On which peninsula of the Scottish mainland will
    you find the nearest point to Ireland?

9   If you want to be a local councillor in Scotland, how
    old must you be?

10 On which island group is the stone circle called the
    Ring of Brogar?

11 In 1962, which form of transport plied for the last
    time between Auchenshuggle and Dalmuir West on
    the 'number nine' route?

12 Who has an official home at No. 6 Charlotte Square
    in Edinburgh?

GAME 10

1 Is England nearer France than the centre of Perth is to the middle of Dundee?

2 In the cartoon strip, do 'Maw and Paw Broon' have just seven children?

3 Would you play a game with the Elgin Marbles?

4 Is the resort of Millport on the south coast of Little Cumbrae?

5 Is there a stream in Dumfries-shire called the Water of Milk?

6 Is it over 100 years since Alexander Graham Bell invented the telephone?

7 Is the port of Lochmaddy on the isle of South Uist?

8 Are broadcasters Tom and Molly Weir brother and sister?

9 The ship of explorer Captain Scott is now at Dundee. Is she the *Endeavour*?

10 Is Prince Charles the Great Steward of Scotland?

11 Do the Pentland Hills overlook the Pentland Firth?

12 Was the *Cutty Sark* tea clipper launched before the story of *Treasure Island* was published?

1 Who was the four-legged hero from Scotland of a 1960 Disney film?

2 Edinburgh and Glasgow each have a major theatre with the same name. What is it?

3 What was the setting of a new Scottish play of 1985 called *The Nutcracker Suite*?

4 Which Scottish actor starred in the film *Comfort and Joy*, and had small roles in *The Killing Fields* and *A Private Function*?

5 In Scottish Gaelic broadcasting, a character known as 'Padraig Post' made his appearance in 1985. By which name do English youngsters know 'Padraig Post'?

6 Two members of the amusing *Scotland the What?* team are Stephen Robertson and George Donald. Who completes the trio?

7 Which village about 6 miles south-east of Forres shares its name with an American city and a popular television soap opera?

8 Television reporter Alan Whicker has been quoted as saying his mother gave him a Scottish first name. What is his first name, in fact? Is it Angus, Colin or Donald?

9 Lectures, readings and concerts were held in the Borders in October 1985, to mark the 150th anniversary of the death of a Borders poet. Who was he?

10 What's the surname of the pop singer and composer known as 'B.A.'?

11 Which theatre in an east-coast town claims to be the 'smallest repertory theatre' in Scotland?

12 What major event was the background to Joe Corrie's 1929 play *In Time of Strife*?

1 Who wrote *The Big Man* – described as the 'most important Scottish novel of 1985'?

2 In August 1984, in Aberdeen, the Queen opened the Queen Elizabeth Bridge over which river?

3 Where was the Princess of Wales described as being 'Charlie's Darling' during a visit in September 1985?

4 There was a big campaign to keep open an industrial works at Gartcosh during the mid-1980s. What kind of industrial works was it?

5 The bedroom suite of which Scottish furniture designer was sold to the Louvre in Paris for £300 000 in 1985?

6 That same year, a picture by John Wootton broke the record price for a picture sold in Scotland. Did it fetch £240 000, £440 000 or £640 000?

7 Which School of Glasgow University saw its new home opened in the Stair Building during the 1980s?

8 In 1985, which Scottish product did Mrs Thatcher admit she likes to sample of an evening?

9 In which year were Regional Council elections last held in Scotland?

10 In 1985, which leading churchman did Archbishop Keith O'Brien succeed in Scotland?

11 In which 'big show' did 6500 children take part in July 1986?

12 In 1985, who was elected President of the Royal Society for the Protection of Birds? Was it Tom Weir, Lord Home or Magnus Magnusson?

GAME 10 GENERAL KNOWLEDGE (1)

1   What's the second-largest island in the Firth of Clyde?

2   Who take precedence in Scotland: earls, marquesses or viscounts?

3   Until the 1980s, which offence was usually called 'malicious mischief' in Scotland?

4   If you go to the East Fortune Museum near Edinburgh, what kind of transport will you see on display?

5   In the popular tongue-twister, who 'dismisseth us'?

6   According to the law, what's the minimum age for a baby-sitter in Scotland?

7   Which Channel Island has the same name as a Scottish shirt?

8   Who wrote the book *Ring of Bright Water*?

9   What does 'Green Stuart' have in common with 'Balmoral' and 'Lord of the Isles'?

10 Where in Scotland are two nuclear power stations next-door to each other?

11 Which famous fictional character is said to have been modelled on Dr Joseph Bell of Edinburgh University?

12 In the Church of Scotland, what was once known as 'the occasion'? Was it marriage, christening or communion?

1   Horse racing: what's the most northerly race-course in Britain?

2   One of these three football clubs does *not* feature a lion on its badge. Which is the odd club out: Aberdeen, Dundee United or Rangers?

3   In which town are the trophies of the late racing driver Jim Clark kept in the 'Jim Clark Memorial Room'?

4   In 1985, which Scottish golfer sank the winning putt to bring the Ryder Cup back to Europe?

5   At which of Scotland's ski centres would you be skiing at the Cairnwell?

6   Which Scottish football personality became a Freeman of Manchester in 1967?

7   Who won what with Troy in 1979 and with Henbit in 1980?

8   Golf: where in Scotland was the Open Championship played in 1984?

9   In summer, what kind of boat can you learn to sail at Glenmore Lodge? (Clue: it's a palindrome.)

10 If you tackled the Spartan Slab, the Quiver Rib and the Crow's Nest Crack in Scotland, what would you be doing?

11 If Glasgow Tigers met Middlesbrough Tigers at Blantyre, what was the sport?

12 How many Scottish League football teams play home matches in Fife?

GAME 10 SCOTS WORDS AND SAYINGS

1 In the Borders, which insect has been called a 'redcoat'?

2 Should you be flattered if I describe you as 'Falkland bred'? And give a reason for your answer!

3 Of which girl's name is Catriona a Gaelic form?

4 Which large sword, once used by Highlanders, takes its name from the Gaelic for 'great sword'?

5 In Central Scotland, which wild flower has been known as 'grannie's thimmles'?

6 Which part of your body is your 'haffet'? Is it your knee, your chest or your temple?

7 What would you do with a 'gundy ball' – play marbles with it, eat it or use it during a game of shinty?

8 In geography, what is a 'strath'?

9 What's the meaning of the saying: 'Better make your feet your friends'?

10 Which county was once called Linlithgowshire?

11 Up until 1975, what was the standard Scots name for town magistrates just below the rank of provost?

12 What was the job of a 'baxter' in Scotland?

1   What is traditionally served with chappit tatties and bashed neeps?

2   What are the two vegetables you need to make 'Rumbledethumps'?

3   Which of Scotland's game birds has a name that begins with a silent letter?

4   Which city is mainly linked with breakfast rolls called 'buttery rowies'?

5   What's the main ingredient of 'Tweed kettle'?

6   According to the rhyme, what will you get if you 'dance tae yer daddie'?

7   Which school of sentimental Scots writers shared its name with a name for a patch of vegetables?

8   What type of food is linked with Dundee – and Madeira?

9   If you make carrageen soup, what's its particular ingredient?

10 What do the French call 'water of life'?

11 Last century and early this century, what kind of food were 'anchor-stocks'? Were they toffees, loaves or eels?

12 Which vegetables were once known as 'Falkirk raisins'?

1   You'll find a town in central Scotland if you rearrange the letters in TIN GIRLS correctly!

2   What was launched at Clydebank on 20 September 1967?

3   Edinburgh has one; Dundee has two; Aberdeen has three. What are they?

4   What major construction project has been under way in recent years at Torness in East Lothian?

5   In which town are the headquarters of Moray District?

6   What was Alistair MacLean's first novel?

7   Still with books, how many stories make up *A Scots Quair*, by Lewis Grassic Gibbon?

8   Which writer, when asked the population of England, is said to have answered: 'Thirty millions, mostly fools'?

9   Which royal duke is also Baron Culloden?

10 Which girl's name is the same as a shrub whose formal name is 'calluna vulgaris' or, sometimes, the 'erica' plant?

11 Who was the last British monarch born in Scotland?

12 What do the letters 'K T' mean, after your name?

ANSWERS

Game 1   Yes or No?

1 No. They're at Edinburgh Castle. 2 Yes. 3 No. It was in 1963 that Sir Alec Douglas-Home became Premier. 4 Yes. For thirty years, from 1589. 5 Yes. 6 No. The nine of diamonds has the nickname. 7 No. It's north-east of Iona. 8 Yes. 9 No. It's in Central Region. 10 Yes. It was about 3 imperial pints. 11 Yes. The Dee. 12 Yes.

Game 1   Entertainment

1 The violin. 2 The Eurythmics. 3 Sir James Barrie. 4 Private Fraser. 5 Donald – in 'Donald, Where's Yer Troosers?' 6 The Duchess of Gloucester. 7 The Television and Radio Industries Club (2 points) of Scotland. 8 In Scottish country dancing – it's a popular dance. 9 Five (six people form a set in this dance). 10 Jimmy Mack. 11 *Old Gold* is the programme – top-selling records from years gone by. 12 No. She was an eagle, in Scottish Opera's production of Janáček's *From the House of the Dead*.

Game 1   Place the Place

1 Balmoral. 2 Brodick. 3 Dumbarton. 4 Mull (the galleon is in Tobermory Bay). 5 Inveraray. 6 Haddington (East Lothian was once called 'Haddingtonshire'). 7 The Palace of Holyroodhouse. 8 Loch Morar. 9 Perth. 10 Peterhead. 11 Glamis Castle. 12 Kilmarnock.

Game 1   General Knowledge (1)

1 Brodick Castle. 2 Green ('In pastures green He leadeth me'). 3 James Ogilvy. 4 Caithness (at Dunnet Head). 5 Ardrossan. 6 Clan Murray. 7 Jacobites. 8 James II – so nicknamed because of a mark on his face. 9 The nineteenth century (from 1813 till 1873). 10 On 'Sula' (2 points) – in the book of the same name. 11 The legal profession. The Lay Observer looks into how the Law

Society of Scotland has dealt with complaints. 12 It's a local newspaper, dating back to 1885.

Game 1   Sports
1 The Premier Division. 2 Boxing. 3 Swimming.
4 Rugby Union. Scotland lost 28–22. 5 The European international championship. 6 The (Embassy) World Indoor Bowls Championship. 7 Dumbarton FC.
8 American football. 9 Golf – they're names of types of clubs. 10 Tom Watson. 11 The Great (1 point) Cumbrae (1 point). 12 At Murrayfield (2 points) – playing for Wales in a celebrated rugby international, he scored with a Herculean kick in the dying seconds to win points that defeated Scotland 19–18.

Game 1   Scots Words and Sayings
1 A thatched cottage. 2 Leapfrog. Children's caps were piled on top of the 'frog's' back till someone knocked them over with their leap. 3 The kilt. 4 Pigs. 5 A runaway, or irregular marriage. 6 Stormy or cold and wet weather. 7 A girl (can also mean a woman of worthless character). 8 A hearing. 9 A (light naval) gun. 10 You take the rough with the smooth. 11 The kestrel. 12 Field.

Game 1   Food and Drink
1 A herring or kipper (1 point for 'fish'). 2 An egg.
3 Black (2 points) bun. 4 Because it was boiled in a cloth or 'clout'. 5 (Arbroath) smokies. 6 Eat them. They're chewy sweets in lots of flavours, developed last century. 7 Cabbages and potatoes (with cream and seasoning). 8 16. 9 A gooseberry. 10 Triangular (cut out of a round with the outer edge usually scalloped).
11 Whisky. 12 'parritch' or 'porridge'.

Game 1   General Knowledge (2)
1 Durness. 2 Two from: Foundation, General and Credit. 3 Just over 500. 4 Montreal. McGill University was founded there. 5 The Secretary of State for Scotland.

6 Your pound note. There's no toll charge for motor
bikes. 7 Army barracks. 8 The Isle of May. 9 Just over
50 000 – 50 373 miles at the latest count.
10 Aberchirder. 11 The letter 'R'. 12 Prince Charles.

Game 2 Yes or No?

1 Yes. Burke and Hare strangled or choked their victims,
then sold the bodies to medical science. 2 Yes. 3 No.
It's reckoned to be the oldest surviving collection of Scots
fiddle music. 4 Yes. 5 Yes. James Hepburn, Earl of
Bothwell. 6 No. It's in Dunfermline District. 7 No. West
Hartlepool. 8 Yes. At 1160 feet above sea level, it's
nearly 50 feet higher. 9 No. King Edward I's was.
10 Yes. 11 No. It was 1924. 12 No. The Duchess of
Rothesay is the Princess of Wales.

Game 2 Entertainment

1 Ballet – as principal dancer with the Scottish Ballet.
2 Carolina. 3 The late Chic Murray. 4 Kathleen
Garscadden – pioneer broadcaster as Auntie Kathleen of
Children's Hour to generations of young listeners.
5 'Johnnie Cope'. 6 'I Belong to Glasgow'. 7 Robbie
Coltrane. 8 Lerwick in Shetland – home of Radio
Shetland. 9 Albert Square. 10 Jack House. 11 'Flower of
Scotland'. 12 James Herriot – the vet of *All Creatures
Great and Small* fame.

Game 2 News of the '80s

1 Prisons. 2 Mr John Smith, MP. 3 Gleneagles Hotel in
Perthshire. 4 (Sir Kenneth) Alexander – Chancellor of
Aberdeen University. (Note: You must know
'Alexander' for 2 points.) 5 The Prince and Princess of
Wales. 6 The Duke of Gloucester (1 point) and the Duke
of Kent (1 point) – the Earl of Inverness being better
known as Prince Andrew, Duke of York. 7 A BBC
Scotland television series of that name – material was
taken away but later returned to the BBC. 8 The
(Scottish) SDP consultative assembly. 9 1982. 10 The

Royal Bank of Scotland. 11 The Scottish Development Agency. 12 Bus services.

Game 2   General Knowledge (1)
1 Hamilton. 2 North-west. 3 Moscow (it's 55° 45' north; Dundee is 56° 28' north). 4 The number of watts indicated. This unit of power was named after James Watt. 5 Hydro-electric power. 6 Richard (1 point) Hannay (1 point). 7 Canada. 8 Firth of Forth. 9 Firth of Clyde – west of Bute. 10 Mary Queen of Scots' supporters. 11 A.J. (Arthur James) Balfour. 12 Ailsa Craig (2 points) – 1114 feet compared to the 823 feet of Arthur's Seat.

Game 2   Sports
1 Maurice. 2 Four – England, Ireland, Wales, France. 3 Coatbridge. 4 Stenhousemuir. 5 Belle Robertson. 6 Allan Wells. 7 1970 – by the British women's 4 x 800 metres relay team. 8 Norris McWhirter, Editor of the book, who ran for Scotland. 9 You wouldn't (1 point), because it's a type of potato (1 point). 10 Aberdeen – they're the Dons. 11 Fir – the grounds are Firs Park, Fir Park and Firhill. 12 Nineteen.

Game 2   Scots Words and Sayings
1 Shrewd. 2 The time – it's a type of clock. 3 Sweetheart or loved one. 4 Wear it – it's a vest or undershirt. 5 Three. Ben Doon?!! 6 'The Bubblyjock' (or turkey). 7 Yes. 8 Yes. 9 A tadpole. 10 You wouldn't wear it (1 point) because it's a drink that's thought to keep you warm – often whisky (1 point). 11 Your stomach or belly. 12 Kilt.

Game 2   Food and Drink
1 Haggis. 2 French. 3 Leg. 4 Campbeltown Loch. 5 Porridge made with beer. 6 An apple – said locally to have been taken to the district by Crusaders from Palestine. 7 For serving food – it's a serving dish.

8 Whisky. 9 Malt and blend. 10 A raspberry. 11 Pan loaf.
12 Wonder(s). They're types of potato.

Game 2 General Knowledge (2)
1 Montrose. 2 He's 'in his nicht goon'. 3 Edinburgh.
4 The Convention of Scottish Local Authorities. 5 The
grey seal. 6 The National Trust for Scotland (2 points) –
leased to the Nature Conservancy Council. 7 The *Courier*
(of Dundee). (Though the *Courier* does have its 'stop
press' space on page one.) 8 Tobacco (2 points also for
'smoking') – in his 'A Counterblaste to Tobacco'.
9 Synods. 10 Foreign Secretary. 11 The M8.
12 Eighteen.

Game 3 Yes or No?
1 No. It was Archibald. 2 No. It's from the 'Mingulay
Boat Song'. 3 Yes – the basketball side of that name!
4 Yes. 5 No. It was in 1966. 6 Yes. 7 Yes. 8 No. They're
in Paisley. 9 No. 10 No – 470 miles compared to 535
miles from Perth to Plymouth. 11 No. The south-east –
near Dunbar. 12 Yes.

Game 3 Entertainment
1 In the Scottish top twenty – 'Male Stripper' by Man 2
Man, and Westworld's 'Sonic Boom Boy'. 2 *My Music*.
3 Bagpipes. 4 John Byrne. 5 Helen Mirren. 6 August.
7 He was Sir Edward (2 points) Montague Compton
Mackenzie. 8 Sally Magnusson, daughter of Magnus.
9 The bawbee – in 'The Crookit Bawbee'. 10 Naked
(2 points) Radio and Video. 11 David Bellamy – in a
controversy when nature conservation was ranged
against local jobs. 12 The late Robert Wilson.

Game 3 Place the Place
1 Aberfeldy. 2 Dunstaffnage Castle. 3 Fair Isle.
4 Glencoe (scene of the massacre of Clan MacDonald).
5 Grangemouth. 6 Livingston. 7 Ayr. 8 Lochnagar.

9 Loch Katrine. 10 Strathaven. 11 Peebles. 12 The Isle of Lewis.

Game 3   General Knowledge (1)
1 Queen Anne. 2 Chemistry. 3 Rut. 4 Autumn – around October. 5 Loch Tay. 6 Black, yellow and red. 7 John Prebble. 8 European Regional Development Fund. 9 Lord Ross (2 points) of Marnock – formerly Willie Ross MP. 10 Blue (2 points) bonnets. 11 February – on the second day of the month. 12 Thursday.

Game 3   Sports
1 The MBE. 2 A (primary school) headmaster. 3 Glenmore Lodge. 4 Chay Blyth, when trying to set a sailing record between New York and San Francisco. 5 They were beaten 20-0 (2 points) by Stirling Albion in the Scottish Cup. 6 Links Park – home of Montrose (but no points if you answer 'Montrose'!). 7 Thirteen – against Bon Accord (2 points for any answer between eleven and fifteen). 8 July (24th). 9 The thirteenth. 10 Murrayfield. 11 Shooting (2 points) in the small-bore rifle event. 12 Allan Wells.

Game 3   Scots Words and Sayings
1 Mountains. 2 At a wedding – these are names for the old custom of throwing coins for children. 3 A ram (1 point for 'sheep'). 4 The puffin. 5 The Devil. 6 The skylark. 7 Rob or plunder. 8 A Highland reiver. 9 Sheep. 10 Red. 11 Face on. 12 Freckles.

Game 3   Food and Drink
1 Jedburgh – they're toffee 'Jeddart snails'. 2 (Smoked) haddock. 3 Bake them (2 points) – they're made with flour, currants, sugar, margarine and bicarbonate of soda. 4 Buttermilk (2 points) all the week. 5 When working with butter – it's a kind of small wooden bat. 6 A large bannock. 7 A chicken or fowl. 8 Trout – a growing market for fish farmers. 9 Kippers ('herring' is

also worth 2 points). 10 At least 35 per cent (2 points for 30-40 per cent). 11 At least 25 per cent (2 points for 20-30 per cent). 12 Fourteen.

Game 3   General Knowledge (2)

1 Aberfeldy. 2 Grampian Region. 3 James. 4 East Kilbride and Eastwood District Councils. 5 The *Observer*. In Stirling, the local *Observer* comes out on Wednesdays and Fridays. 6 The winding course of the River Forth in this area. 7 The Antonine Wall. 8 Irvine. 9 Highland Region – it's near Loch Carron. 10 Eighteen. 11 The Earl of Erroll. 12 Loch Long.

Game 4   Yes or No?

1 No. They're a folk band. 2 Yes. 3 Yes – King Olav. 4 Yes. 5 No. It's a pig, especially a young one. 6 Yes. 7 No. It was founded by a man – Archie Charteris. 8 No. It would be amateur theatre, since the SCDA is the Scottish Community Drama Association. 9 Yes. That's the home of the Scottish Police College. 10 Yes – 39 compared with 44. 11 Yes. 12 No. That's the code for Aberdeen.

Game 4   Entertainment

1 As a conductor. 2 As ballerina Moira Shearer. 3 Forestry, after graduating as a BSc from Aberdeen University. 4 I.M. (Both must be correct for any points.) 5 Going to the cinema (around five million seats filled – about twice as many as football admissions). 6 All are titles of plays by James Bridie. 7 Jimmy Logan. 8 Billy Connolly. 9 The strathspey. 10 Tom and Jack (1 point each). 11 Jimmie MacGregor (and Robin Hall is still to the fore on our airwaves as well). 12 Roger Whittaker.

Game 4   News of the '80s

1 Rector of Glasgow University. 2 Barlinnie Prison in Glasgow (in a dispute about the number of prisoners the prison should hold). 3 Loch Lomond. 4 *Fiddler on the*

Roof. 5 The 800th anniversary. 6 (Domestic) rates. 7 The telephone engineers strike . . . the NCU is the National Communications Union. 8 The Queen Mother was taken to hospital from Castle of Mey in Caithness after 'discomfort' in her throat from a fishbone. 9 *Rupert* was Anne's yacht, in which she returned to Scotland after a double sea crossing of the Atlantic. 10 Minister of State (2 points) at the Scottish Office. 11 A teacher. He has been General Secretary of the EIS. 12 Defence Secretary.

Game 4   General Knowledge (1)
1 Kingston Bridge. 2 'My heart's in the Highlands a-chasing the deer'. 3 Rikki Fulton. 4 1782 – and the new umbrella came from Paris. 5 Your granny – as in 'Ye Canna Shove Yer Granny Off a Bus'! 6 St Peter's (2 points) in Rome. 7 The national anthem – in the eighteenth century. 8 'Shoes Were For Sunday'. 9 'Come saddle your horses and call up your men' (1 point), from 'Bonnie Dundee' (1 point). 10 Two from: the Dee, the Ewe and the Eye (which is actually the Eye Water). 11 The Laird O' Cockpen. 12 As The Corries.

Game 4   Sports
1 'Fute-ball and golfe'. 2 It was the last match in the British Championship series. 3 As Jocky Wilson (2 points), top darts player. 4 Murrayfield. 5 Rugby Union. 6 Dundee and Dundee United. 7 Curling. 'Sooping' is sweeping ahead of the stone with the broom. 8 It was the first Premier Division goal. 9 Bowls. 10 A football match. In the Highland League, Inverness Clachnacuddin are the Lilywhites and Forres Mechanics are the Can-Cans. 11 They're all flies (2 points) used in (trout) fishing. 12 Queen's Park.

Game 4   Scots Words and Sayings
1 Ferryman. 2 On your legs – they were leggings or gaiters. 3 Gaelic. 4 A gold coin (from the time of King James V). 5 It showed the king wearing a bonnet. 6 A

Donald – it's a Lowlands hill of 2000 feet or more. A Corbett (*not* named after Ronnie!) is between 2500 and 3000 feet, and a Munro is 3000 feet or over. 7 Hell. 8 Rain. 9 Blind man's buff. 10 A (licensed) beggar. 11 A blacksmith. 12 To wake people (2 points) by knocking on the doors or windows of those who paid a small fee.

Game 4   Food and Drink

1 Pancake Day or Shrove Tuesday. 2 Scotland. 3 Raspberries. 4 Porridge. 5 An oatcake, scone or roll. 6 A whiting or haddock (2 points) cured with smoke of green wood, peat or turf. 7 An oatcake. 8 '. . . girdle'. 9 Impatient or anxious. 10 A pan drop (1 point for 'peppermint'). 11 Onions and oatmeal (2 points), butter or dripping, and seasoning. 12 Dessert. It's made with fruit and jelly.

Game 4   General Knowledge (2)

1 Linlithgow. 2 The 'Wolf of Badenoch' – Alexander Stewart. 3 Strathclyde. 4 Prince Charles Edward Stuart. 5 The Ochils. 6 Wigtownshire. 7 Sir Walter Scott. The *Chronicles* included *The Two Drovers* and *The Highland Widow*. 8 Prestwick Airport. 9 The Solway Firth. 10 Just one (2 points) – Dumfries and Galloway. 11 Central Region. 12 Twice – to Marjory Bowes and then, at around fifty, to the teenage Margaret Stewart.

Game 5   Yes or No?

1 Yes. 2 No. He was born in Edinburgh, but went to Sandyknowe at about two years old to recover from infantile paralysis. 3 No. They're deer. 4 Yes – the Royal Caledonian Curling Club. 5 No. It's off the west side. 6 No. Selkirk. 7 Yes. 8 Yes. It's a whirlpool. 9 No. It was Charles Lamb. 10 No. They're at Ingliston, near Edinburgh. 11 Yes. 12 Yes.

Game 5   Entertainment
1 Jessie Kesson. 2 Glasgow (he later lived in Perth and Arbroath in his youth). 3 'Comin' Through the Rye'.
4 The Family Ness. 5 A strip ('I'm the Quine who did the Strip at Inverurie' is the song). 6 The Reith Lectures.
7 Ice-cream firms. 8 1984 – in October. 9 Sean Connery.
10 (Peter) Maxwell Davies. 11 S. 12 Lulu.

Game 5   Place the Place
1 The River Clyde. 2 Dunnottar Castle. 3 Lanark. 4 (The summit of) Ben Nevis. 5 Dunbar. 6 Langholm. 7 Oban.
8 The Forth Rail Bridge. 9 Portree (on Skye). 10 John O'Groats. 11 The Castle of Mey. 12 The Burrell Collection in Glasgow's Pollok Country Park.

Game 5   General Knowledge (1)
1 Jenny Geddes. 2 Fourteenth century (in 1320). 3 Latin.
4 A waterfall. 5 Aberdeen. 6 11 a.m. 7 Edinburgh University. 8 Hebrides. 9 Islay. 10 Wick. 11 Rockall.
12 King James VI (to the English Parliament in 1607).

Game 5   Sports
1 1967. 2 Nairn Golf Club. 3 The rugby union international between England and Scotland. 4 Two from: East Fife, East Stirlingshire and Queen of the South (note: 'Heart of Midlothian' is not a point of the compass). 5 Darts. 6 Celtic. 7 Prince Philip, Duke of Edinburgh. 8 Old Trafford (2 points), home of Manchester United. 9 1985. 10 The UEFA Cup.
11 Methil, home of East Fife. 12 Airdrie(onians).

Game 5   Scots Words and Sayings
1 It's Edinburgh. 2 Make music with it: it's an accordion or melodeon. 3 A soldier. 4 A round tower (2 points) with inner and outer walls – a 'Pictish castle'. 5 A brewer.
6 Getting married. 7 The chanter. 8 Arbroath. 9 A cup, bowl or goblet. 10 French (from *tasse*, meaning a cup).
11 You flatter them. 12 A gossip.

Game 5   Food and Drink
1 Hare soup. 2 A dram. 3 Sir Compton Mackenzie.
4 Todday. 5 Beer. 6 Porridge. 7 Dundee. 8 'Willie (2
points) brew'd a peck o' maut' is the song. 9 More (about
a tenth more). 10 The Forth. 11 A shellfish. 12 The
whortleberry, or bilberry.

Game 5   General Knowledge (2)
1 Maidens. 2 Robert Burns. 3 Nicholas Fairbairn MP.
4 The North Sea oil (and gas) industry. 5 England.
6 Norway. 7 Balmoral Castle. 8 It's right in the middle of
a city (2 points) . . . in Edinburgh. 9 The Forth Road
Bridge . . . its north pier stands on the rock. 10 The
Queen Mother. 11 Two. 12 Dundee.

Game 6   Yes or No?
1 Yes – after a gardener called William Forsyth, of Old
Meldrum. 2 No. It's downstream. 3 Yes. 4 Yes. 5 Yes.
6 Yes. 7 Yes – excellent, beautiful or pleasant. 8 No.
It's the most southerly point of Bute. 9 No. Crannachan
is a dessert. 10 Yes. 11 Yes. It can be the gullet
(oesophagus) or windpipe (trachea). 12 No. In summer,
on or around 1 August.

Game 6   Entertainment
1 Moira Anderson. 2 John McGlynn. 3 Islay (from 'In
Praise of Islay'). 4 Janice. 5 Janet. 6 Football, or
'the fitba' game' in 'Fitba' Crazy'. 7 Jimmy Krankie.
8 1952. 9 The Beechgrove Garden. 10 A teacher.
11 Glasgow. 12 Disc jockey Gerry MacKenzie.

Game 6   News of the '80s
1 Shetland. 2 Dounreay. 3 France. 4 Revaluation. 5 The
(story of the) Highlands and Islands Development
Board. 6 It became cheaper – the basic rate down from
13p to 12p. 7 David Steel MP. 8 Edinburgh. 9 Donald
Stewart. 10 Gorillas at Edinburgh Zoo. 11 Four Roman
forts (2 points), or the remains of them, were detected in

an aerial survey; and after the dry 1984 summer they could be seen clearly from the air. 12 The economy (2 points) of Scotland.

Game 6   General Knowledge (1)
1 'Mull of Kintyre'. 2 A minister of religion (or a registrar). 3 You like pop music. They are two girls from the west of Scotland who found success in the record charts. 4 Dumfries and Galloway. 5 The flag of the St Andrew's Cross. 6 The Minch. 7 Central Station. 8 Paisley. 9 Peterhead. 10 The Crinan Canal. 11 'The Red (2 points) Yo-Yo'. 12 In the countryside (2 points). SWRI stands for the Scottish Women's Rural Institute.

Game 6   Sports
1 The 10 000 metres. 2 Snooker. 3 Shinty. 4 1983. 5 Four. 6 Boxing. 7 Hearts – they went down 3-0. 8 Secretary (1 point) of the Royal and Ancient Golf Club (1 point). 9 International skiing, as Britain's top 'downhill' hope. 10 1985. 11 Curling. 12 Hamilton (2 points) Academicals.

Game 6   Scots Words and Sayings
1 A Glengarry. 2 Keeping corn or grain. 3 In a bad mood. 4 Your little finger. 5 A road. 6 To get light – it was a lamp, candlestick or stand for a lamp. 7 The cornflower. 8 Draughts – a 'dambrod' is a draughts-board. 9 Dawn. 10 Your elbow. 11 Church or cell. 12 A crow.

Game 6   Food and Drink
1 A meal chest. 2 The head. 3 A stone on which you baked bannocks on the fire. 4 You take a generous swig of beer (or other drink). 5 Four – it's usually a quarter of a round. 6 A (salt) herring. 7 Sugar, cream of tartar, water and flavourings. 8 Cheeses. 9 As clear as crystal. 10 Biscuits. 11 '. . . silver tassie'. 12 *Treasure Island* by Robert Louis Stevenson.

Game 6   General Knowledge (2)
1 Seil. 2 Dalkeith. 3 'The friendly cow (2 points), all red and white'. From 'The Cow'. 4 The Isle of Man. 5 Nova Scotia. 6 Kirkpatrick. 7 Tweed. 8 For his architecture (2 points), which had a strong Greek influence. 9 The 'thin red line'. 10 In the Crimean (2 points) War. 11 The University of Aberdeen. 12 Berwickshire.

Game 7   Yes or No?
1 Yes. 2 Yes – in 1880. 3 No. It's in Musselburgh. 4 Yes. 5 No. He belonged to Selkirk. 6 Yes. It's also been called the trigger fish of Sumatra. 7 Yes. 8 No. It's in Glasgow. 9 Yes (Kirkpatrick Macmillan). 10 Yes – Sir Robert Watson-Watt. 11 Yes. 12 No. It's about 1800 square miles and Central is 1000 square miles.

Game 7   Entertainment
1 Lawyer or solicitor. 2 Ross Davidson. 3 Hannah Gordon – in the television series of that name. 4 Sean Connery. 5 The late Fulton MacKay. 6 Three (*Ane Satire of the Thrie Estaitis*). 7 *Restless Natives*. 8 Big Country. 9 Allan Ramsay. 10 The Corries. 11 The Citizens' Theatre. 12 Crichton (2 points) dates back to 1902. Peter Pan came along in 1904.

Game 7   Place the Place
1 Drumlanrig Castle. 2 Campbeltown. 3 Dryburgh Abbey. 4 Fort Augustus. 5 Iona. 6 St Andrews. 7 Floors Castle. 8 Lerwick (scene of the Up Helly Aa fire festival and the home of BBC Radio Shetland). 9 The Wallace Monument. 10 Abbotsford (home of Sir Walter Scott). 11 Stranraer. 12 Inverewe Gardens.

Game 7   General Knowledge (1)
1 Tayside Region. 2 70 mph. 3 60 mph. 4 Lord Advocate. 5 France. 6 Nairn. 7 The sweet william – named after William, Duke of Cumberland. 8 The Firth

of Forth. 9 Thomas Carlyle. 10 Ravenscraig. 11 *Old Mortality*. 12 Glasgow.

Game 7   Sports

1 Arsenal. 2 They're all 'Athletics' – Alloa Athletic, Forfar Athletic and Dunfermline Athletic. 3 Greyhound racing. The track closed after over fifty years of greyhound racing. 4 The Commonwealth Games. 5 Curlers! 6 Athletics. The stamp showed an athlete's feet at the starting blocks. 7 You do a somersault. 8 Mr (Robert) Maxwell. 9 Golf. 10 St Johnstone – from Premier Division to Second Division in two years. 11 Zola Budd's (televising of the meeting was cancelled because of local council banners against apartheid). 12 Identity cards.

Game 7   Scots Words and Sayings

1 '. . . babbety'. 2 You're on the road to ruin. 3 Smuggling. 4 Brother-in-law. 5 An owl. 6 The (song) thrush. 7 Midlothian. 8 Stornoway (the 'Long Island' is another name for the Outer Hebrides). 9 It's the document that actually transfers ownership. 10 Honesty is the best policy (the Scots proverb means: 'Long honest, long poor!'). 11 It never rains but it pours. 12 A bay (from the Norse 'vik').

Game 7   Food and Drink

1 A choppin (2 points) was equal to two mutchkins. 2 When you are leaving someone's home – it's a parting cup. 3 Sprats. 4 Angus MacVicar. 5 A soup made with haddock. (1 point for 'fish soup'.) 6 Yes. It was a steak and kidney pie with mussels (or oysters.) 7 Dessert. It's a creamy concoction. 8 No. It was a measure holding a quart. 9 Desperate Dan (in *The Dandy*). 10 '. . . Great chieftain o' the puddin-race!'. 11 F. Marian McNeill, Ena Baxter and Elizabeth Craig. 12 A lang spoon (because, so the saying implied, you had to be on your guard when dealing with a Fife person!).

Game 7 General Knowledge (2)
1 Anstruther. 2 The Royal Air Force. 3 Largo. 4 The
Bass Rock – it's 350 feet high. Dumbarton Rock is 240
feet high. 5 Lothian and Borders Regions. 6 The Kelso
Laddie. 7 The (fifth) Earl of Angus (who earned the
nickname for the part he played leading to the hanging of
King James III's favourites). 8 A puffer (2 points) –
named the 'Vital Spark'. 9 Insch. 10 King Charles I. 11
'To a Louse' was the poem – so 2 points for 'louse'.
12 When words of persuasion failed, she would offer a
kiss to win the recruit.

Game 8 Yes or No?
1 Yes. 2 Yes. 3 No. She writes in the *Sunday Post*. 4 Yes.
5 Yes. 6 No. He is Chancellor of the University of
Strathclyde. 7 No. He was born in London. 8 Yes. 9 Yes
– 424 feet higher. 10 No. Nearly two out of three full-
time teachers are women. 11 No. She was eight when she
broadcast for the BBC in Scotland. 12 No. It's to the
east.

Game 8 Entertainment
1 Archie MacPherson. 2 Music, as a composer. 3 *Peter
Pan*. 4 Jim MacLeod. 5 Piano. 6 They're all names of
tunes for reels (2 points) in Scottish country dancing.
7 (Cilla) Fisher and (Artie) Trezise. 8 Charles Coborn
(real name Colin McCallum, whose father belonged to
Inverness). 9 Robert Kemp. 10 Skiffle. 11 Tommy
Morgan. 12 Dave Willis.

Game 8 News of the '80s
1 Scottish Director of the National Coal Board (as it was
then). 2 Mr Gorbachev. 3 A cycling race. 4 1984.
5 Pound notes. 6 The BBC Scottish Symphony
Orchestra. 7 At Glasgow – in November 1985. 8 The
Queen. 9 Three. 10 Mr Donald Dewar MP. 11 Lord
Grimond (formerly Mr Jo Grimond). Either for 2 points.
12 Andrew Carnegie.

Game 8   General Knowledge (1)

1 Perth. 2 They were (successful) rock groups of the time. 3 Loch Linnhe. 4 (Thomas) Telford. 5 Orkney – they're causeways built in the Second World War to protect the waters of Scapa Flow. 6 The Royal Scots (or 'The Royal Regiment'). 7 The M9. 8 Two (2 points) – Strathclyde, and Borders. 9 Arran. 10 Mull. 11 Galashiels. 12 Ardnamurchan Point – the places mentioned are the northern, southern, eastern and western extremities of the Scottish mainland.

Game 8   Sports

1 The Kelvin Hall, Glasgow. 2 August (2 points) has the start of the grouse-shooting season. 3 Perth. 4 In 1978 (1 point), to support Scotland in football's World Cup (1 point) finals. 5 Hearts (Heart of Midlothian). 6 The boy was declared to have lost 'amateur' status as an athlete – but he was later reinstated! 7 Two points (16 points against 14). 8 Sixteen – there were eleven footballers, twelve shinty players and fifteen in the rugby union team. 9 Trampolining. 10 Fishing – it was a small net to catch fish lying behind stones in rivers. 11 Brechin City. 12 The Glasgow Open.

Game 8   Scots Words and Sayings

1 Edinburgh. 2 Kirkcaldy. 3 A top hat. 4 The common, or pipistrelle, bat. 5 Because it's a mammal, not a bird. 6 The pine marten. 7 Midges. 8 A (rounded) hill (and can also be an artificial mound or hillock). 9 The lilac. 10 Curling. 11 The Lochaber axe – a kind of pole-axe or halberd. 12 It was a leather strap, made in Lochgelly, for punishment in school.

Game 8   Food and Drink

1 Scampi. 2 'Some hae meat and cannae eat'. 3 ('The king sits) in Dunfermline town'. 4 Minced meat. 5 Whisky, eggs and sugar. 6 Pancakes. 7 A soup. 8 Oats. 9 Drink it

(it's a 'cocktail' of oatmeal, milk and water). 10 Forfar.
11 Mutton. 12 Crab.

Game 8   General Knowledge (2)
1 Leadhills. 2 It spells the same forwards and backwards
– it's a palindrome. 3 Painting. 4 The motor trade – the
bodies are the Society of Motor Manufacturers and
Traders, and the Scottish Motor Trade Association.
5 Bridge of. 6 Three (2 points) – Prince Charles, Prince
Andrew and Prince Edward. 7 Your shin – it's Loch
Shin. 8 St John Ogilvie. 9 Captain Kidd. 10 Guns (2
points) made for King James IV. 11 Fife. 12 The stoat.

Game 9   Yes or No?
1 Yes. 2 No. Its 850th. 3 No. He was second. 4 No.
Three out of ten do. 5 Yes – on 27 January in 1926.
6 Yes. 7 No. There are seven. 8 Yes. 9 Yes. By about
1700 square miles. 10 No. The 'Cobbler' is just another
name for Ben Arthur. 11 No. It's a wheelbarrow. 12 Yes.
Some of our peat bogs are fine examples of an ancient
landscape.

Game 9   Entertainment
1 Gordon Jackson – in the television series *Upstairs,
Downstairs*. 2 Alastair Sim. George Cole played a
Cockney wartime evacuee in the West End play *Cottage
To Let*, thanks to Alastair. 3 Phyllis Logan. 4 *Another
Time, Another Place*. 5 Tom Conti. 6 Russ Abbot. 7 The
Commonwealth Games (2 points) Appeal Fund. 8 Midge
Ure. 9 Ronnie Corbett (the Ronnie Corbett Golf Classic).
10 Captain Pugwash. 11 Country and western music.
12 Billy Connolly.

Game 9   Place the Place
1 Gatehouse of Fleet. 2 George Square in Glasgow.
3 Drumochter Pass. 4 The Isle of Canna. 5 Port Glasgow.
6 Helensburgh. 7 Traquair House. 8 The Braemar

(Highland) Gathering. 9 The Isle of Jura. 10 Thurso.
11 Lossiemouth. 12 The Grey Mare's Tail waterfall.

Game 9   General Knowledge (1)
1 Paisley shawls. 2 George III. 3 A sheep. 4 The North
Sea oil (and gas) industry. 5 Fort. 6 Dundee University.
7 Orkney. It's at Kirkwall. 8 Lady Helen Windsor – the
Earl is the Duke of Kent's elder son. 9 Four (Aberdeen,
Dundee, Edinburgh and Glasgow). 10 (Robert Louis)
Stevenson. 11 Culzean Castle. 12 The Duke of Hamilton.

Game 9   Sports
1 Chess. 2 Secretary of the Scottish Football League.
3 (Tom) McKean. 4 The skip. 5 Gliding. 6 The Freuchie
cricket team reached the final at Lords of the national
village cricket competition – the first Scottish team to do
so – and won. 7 Golf. There's a fine course there.
8 Strathclyde Country Park. 9 The goal. 10 Dundee
United. 11 Rugby (2 points) union. 12 Hamilton (2
points) Academicals. They play at Douglas Park.

Game 9   Scots Words and Sayings
1 You wouldn't have liked it (1 point) because it was a
wound or cut in the face (1 point). 2 You're always
delaying action. 3 A rabbit. 4 Mod. 5 Capercailzie.
6 Parliament. 7 The Immortal Memory. 8 It was a minor
battle in which Royalists beat some Covenanters.
9 It's for pulling up turnips. 10 Jack Frost. 11 It's a
country dance. 12 Old news.

Game 9   Food and Drink
1 The blackcurrant. 2 Wine – it was a case for holding
wine (a cellaret). 3 Pitlochry (at Faskally). 4 Iron (they
were flat cooking utensils highly regarded by King James
VI). 5 Salmon. 6 'Coulter's Candy'. 7 The washing-up.
The jawbox was the sink. 8 The Borders, particularly
Peebles and Galashiels. 9 Green. 10 Hallowe'en.
11 Scampo. 12 A (hard-boiled) egg – that's Scotch egg.

Game 9   General Knowledge (2)
1 Peterhead. 2 Two years (under 'solemn procedure').
3 '. . . in the gloaming'. 4 The Clydesdale. 5 Margaret,
heir to the Scottish throne – she died as a child on her
way here. 6 A ward. 7 Yes. 8 The Mull of Kintyre.
9 Twenty-one. 10 Orkney. It's on the mainland of
Orkney. 11 The (Glasgow) trams. 12 The Secretary of
State for Scotland.

Game 10   Yes or No?
1 Yes. 17 miles compared to 21 miles. 2 No. Eight.
3 No. They're a collection of ancient Greek sculptures.
4 No. It's on the Great Cumbrae. 5 Yes. 6 Yes. He
patented the telephone in 1876. 7 No. It's on North Uist.
8 Yes. 9 No. She's *Discovery*. 10 Yes. 11 No. The hills are
near Edinburgh, and the Firth is off the north coast.
12 Yes. In 1869, fourteen years before *Treasure Island*.

Game 10   Entertainment
1 Greyfriars Bobby. 2 The King's Theatre. 3 The Special
Unit of Barlinnie Prison. 4 Bill Paterson. 5 As cartoon
character 'Postman Pat'. 6 Buff Hardie. 7 Dallas.
8 Donald. 9 James Hogg. 10 Robertson. 11 The Byre
Theatre (2 points) in St Andrews. 12 (The life of a
mining family during) the General Strike.

Game 10   News of the '80s
1 William McIlvanney. 2 The Dee. 3 On the 'Charlie'
oil field (2 points) production platform in the North Sea.
4 It was a steel mill. 5 Charles Rennie Mackintosh.
6 £240 000. 7 The School of Law. 8 Whisky. She made
this revelation during a visit to a distillery in Scotland.
9 1986. 10 Cardinal (Gordon) Gray. 11 The
Commonwealth Games opening ceremony. 12 Magnus
Magnusson.

Game 10   General Knowledge (1)
1 Bute. 2 Marquesses, then earls, then viscounts.

3 Vandalism – a law in 1980 created the offence of vandalism. 4 Aircraft – East Fortune is the home of the Museum of Flight. 5 The Leith Police. 6 Sixteen. 7 Sark. 8 Gavin Maxwell wrote this famous tale about otters. 9 They're all tartans. 10 At Hunterston. They are Hunterston 'A' and Hunterston 'B'. 11 Sherlock Holmes. 12 Communion – the Sacrament of the Lord's Supper.

Game 10   Sports
1 Perth – at Scone (either name for 2 points). 2 Aberdeen is the odd one out. 3 Duns. 4 Sam Torrance. 5 Glenshee. 6 Sir Matt Busby, a great manager of Manchester United. 7 Jockey Willie Carson (1 point) won the Derby (1 point) on these horses. 8 St Andrews. 9 A kayak – spelling the same backwards as forwards. 10 You'd be climbing. These are climbing routes in the Glencoe area. 11 Speedway. 12 Four (2 points) – East Fife, Dunfermline, Cowdenbeath and Raith Rovers.

Game 10   Scots Words and Sayings
1 A ladybird. 2 You should be flattered (1 point). It means you have good manners (1 point), and has its origins in the days when the Royal court was at Falkland Palace in Fife. 3 Catherine. 4 Claymore. 5 Foxglove. 6 Your temple. 7 Eat it – it's a toffee. 8 A river valley. 9 Get away as fast as you can; run for your life. 10 West Lothian. 11 Bailies. 12 A baker.

Game 10   Food and Drink
1 Haggis. 2 Potatoes and cabbages (1 point each). 3 Ptarmigan. 4 Aberdeen. 5 Salmon. 6 'A fishie (1 point) in a little dishie (1 point)'. 7 The 'kailyard school'. 8 Cake. 9 Seaweed. 10 Whisky (*eau de vie*). 11 Long loaves. It's thought they took their name from a resemblance to part of an anchor. 12 Green peas.

Game 10 General Knowledge (2)

1 Stirling. 2 The liner *Queen Elizabeth II* or *QE2*. 3 The letter 'E'. 4 A nuclear power station. 5 Elgin. 6 *HMS Ulysses*. 7 Three. 8 Thomas Carlyle. 9 The Duke of Gloucester. 10 Heather. 11 Charles I. 12 You're a Knight of the Thistle.

You may also enjoy these BBC quizbooks:

FOOD AND DRINK
with a foreword by Chris Kelly

Inspired by the BBC's *Food and Drink* experts, try your hand at answering the hundreds of ingenious and testing questions crammed into this book, and reward yourself for a correct reply with one of Michael Barry's or Michael Smith's mouthwatering two-minute dishes, or Jill Goolden's or Oz Clarke's exotic cocktails.

- Who wrote 'Candy is dandy, but liquor is quicker'?
- What type of milk is mozzarella cheese traditionally made from?
- Which country has more breweries than any other nation?

With rounds on food and literature, food and the movies, food and music, there's something here for all tastes.

TELLY ADDICTS 2
with a foreword by Noel Edmonds

A second book of teasers from Noel Edmonds' top BBC quizshow. How do you match up against the families on *Telly Addicts?*

- In which series does a computer called Holly appear?
- Name the first chairman of *Call My Bluff*.
- What is the ARP warden in *Dad's Army* called?
- On which American show was Judy Carne the 'sock it to me' girl?

Have fun at home answering these and hundreds more questions from the show, and discover who's the real Telly Addict in your family . . .

THE ARCHERS

Most Archers' fans remember the night Grace Archer was killed rescuing her horse from a stable fire, but what was the horse's name?

● How well do you know the Archers' family tree? Who was Doris Archer's brother? Or Mrs Perkins' son-in-law? Which is the elder twin, Kenton or Shula?

● Can you name all four actors who have played the part of Dan Archer? Who are the real life father and daughter who play a father and daughter in the series?

You'll find the answers to these and hundreds more questions on Ambridge and the Archers in this latest BBC Quizbook.

FIRST CLASS
with a foreword by Debbie Greenwood

● Which woollen hat sounds like a fruit?
● What is Prince's full name?
● Subtract the year of Magna Carta from the year of the battle of Waterloo, and what number are you left with?
● What would you do with a Sopwith Camel?

First Class, BBC 1's popular, fast-moving quiz hosted by Debbie Greenwood, is now on the screen on Saturday evenings.

Have fun answering hundreds of questions from the show – on general knowledge, pop music, the movies, sport, and news of the 80s.

Whether you're aged eight or eighty, you're bound to find something here to test your wits and ingenuity!

TRIVIA TEST MATCH
with a foreword by Brian Johnston

The book of Radio 4's hilarious quiz show in which
teams captained by Tim Rice and Willie Rushton are
bowled questions of the utmost triviality on all possible
topics by Brian Johnston.
Loosely based on the laws of cricket, the book comes
provided with a set of rules (though no one really
understands them, least of all the umpire) and a score
card for the really competitive player.

BEAT THE TEACHER
with a foreword by Bruno Brookes

- A miller mills, a robber robs, and a farmer farms.
  What does a farrier do?
- What is the least possible number of throws it takes
  to win a double four with two dice?
- A sliced loaf of bread has 17 slices in it. How many
  half sandwiches can you make?
- Where do you find the bottom at the top?

Beat the Teacher, BBC tv's popular quiz presented by
Bruno Brookes, gives kids the chance to pit their wits
against their teacher – and usually win!
In this book you'll find hundreds of brain-teasing
questions, logical puzzles and riddles devised by Clive
Doig, with a little help from viewers. Try them at home
and see who fares best: parents or children.
(Grandparents, aunts and uncles can have a go too!)
There's a special grid for scoring each game, so you can
keep a running tally of your total.